Patron Saint of the New World:
Spanish American Colonial Images of
St. Joseph

The exhibition "Patron Saint of the New World: Spanish American Colonial Images of St. Joseph" was made possible through the generosity of Paul and Barbara Henkels.

Curators:
Barbara von Barghahn
Joseph F. Chorpenning, O.S.F.S.
Christopher Chadwick Wilson

Exhibition dates:
University Gallery, Saint Joseph's University, February 21–March 27, 1992

Copyright © 1992 Saint Joseph's University. All rights reserved.
Copyright to works in this exhibition is retained by their owners.
Second printing—1996
ISBN 0-916101-11-8

Designed, typeset, and printed by
Saint Joseph's University Press, Philadelphia
Member, Association of Jesuit University Presses.

Library of Congress Cataloging–in–Publication Data
Patron Saint of the New World : Spanish American colonial images of
    St. Joseph / edited by Joseph Francis Chorpenning : with a preface
    by Santiago Sebastián López.
        p.   cm.
    Catalogue of an exhibition held at Saint Joseph's University,
February 21-March 27, 1992.
    Includes bibliographical references.
    ISBN 0-916101-11-8
    1. Art. Spanish colonial--Latin America--Exhibitions. 2. Joseph,
Saint--Art--Exhibitions. 3. Jesus Christ--Family--Art--Exhibitions.
I. Chorpenning, Joseph F.
N6502.2.P37   1995
755' .63' 09807474811--dc20   95-6641
                                                                  CIP

Cover photo: *St. Joseph Walking with the Christ Child*.
School of Cuzco (Peru). 18th century.
Private collection, Washington, D.C.

Patron Saint of the New World:
Spanish American Colonial Images of St. Joseph

Edited by
JOSEPH F. CHORPENNING, O.S.F.S.

With a Preface by
SANTIAGO SEBASTIÁN LÓPEZ

SAINT JOSEPH'S UNIVERSITY PRESS
PHILADELPHIA, PENNSYLVANIA

Table of Contents

PREFACE vii
   Santiago Sebastián López

INTRODUCTION 1
   Joseph F. Chorpenning, O.S.F.S.

ESSAYS

1. "St. Teresa of Ávila's Holy Patron:
   Teresian Sources for the Image of St. Joseph
   in Spanish American Colonial Art" 5
   Christopher Chadwick Wilson

2. "Just Man, Husband of Mary, and
   Guardian of Christ: St. Joseph's Life
   and Virtues in the Spirituality of
   St. Francis de Sales" 19
   Joseph F. Chorpenning, O.S.F.S.

3. "From Prince to Sun King:
   The Image of St. Joseph in Spain
   and the New World" 31
   Barbara von Barghahn

CATALOGUE OF THE EXHIBITION 40

BIOBIBLIOGRAPHICAL NOTES 55
   Joseph F. Chorpenning, O.S.F.S.

SUGGESTIONS FOR FURTHER READING 59
   Christopher Chadwick Wilson

CONTRIBUTORS AND EXHIBITION CURATORS...61

Preface

In mid-January of this year, I was in Washington, D.C., as a guest of George Washington University at the international conference "Portugal and Spain of the Navigators: The Age of Exploration." On this occasion I had the opportunity to meet the North American scholars Barbara von Barghahn, Christopher Wilson, and Joseph Chorpenning, who, with their essays in this volume, offer an appreciation of the present exhibition "Patron Saint of the New World: Spanish American Colonial Images of Saint Joseph." Fr. Chorpenning invited me to write a preface for the catalogue. Hence I write with a swift pen because of the printer's deadline.

In the first place, I congratulate Saint Joseph's University, Philadelphia's Jesuit university, for taking the welcome initiative of sponsoring this exhibition on the occasion of the Quincentenary of the Discovery of America. Thus the words of the sixteenth-century Milanese Dominican friar Isidore de Isolani will be fulfilled: "The Holy Spirit will not cease to move the hearts of all the faithful throughout the domain of the Church on earth until St. Joseph is exalted with new and greater devotion, monasteries are built and churches are raised up in his honor, with his feasts being celebrated and all petitions being resolutely offered and commended to him."

Private devotion to St. Joseph existed in Christianity from the earliest centuries of the Church. However, in the West his cult began to emerge in the ninth century and became widespread three centuries later. It was necessary to wait until the fifteenth century for the first books dedicated to the diffusion of his cult to be written. Preeminent among the authors who took up their pens to write about St. Joseph was Jean Gerson who wrote the long Latin poem *Josephina*, in which he celebrates the virtues and dignity of this saint and proclaims him patron of the family, of workers, and of the dying. During this same period St. Joseph's cult was promoted at the popular level by preachers, among whom the Dominican friar from Valencia St. Vincent Ferrer holds primacy of place.

At the beginning of the sixteenth century, Isidore de Isolani wrote his classic work, *Summa of the Gifts of St. Joseph*, in which St. Joseph is presented as the patron of the Church on earth. In this same century Spanish theologians and mystics such as St. Teresa of Ávila, St. Peter of Alcántara, Bernardino de Laredo, Andrés de Soto, and Francisco Suárez undertook to exalt St. Joseph. Devotion to St. Joseph also spread to the recently discovered New World, with the result that in 1555 New Spain (Mexico) was placed under the patronage of St. Joseph.

In the seventeenth century it was the turn of France's Catholic authors to exalt St. Joseph: Cardinal Bérulle, Bourgoing, Gibieuf, Bossuet, and, especially, St. Francis de Sales. Francis de Sales dedicated his book *Treatise on the Love of God* to St. Joseph. Moreover, he shared his deep personal devotion to St. Joseph with St. Jane Frances de Chantal, with whom he founded the Order of the Visitation of Holy Mary, which was instrumental in disseminating the cult of the husband of Mary. In 1624 Canada was placed under the patronage of St. Joseph.

After the eighteenth-century crisis in devotion to St. Joseph, there was a renewal in the nineteenth century, with the new studies of the Spaniard Manuel María de Sanlucár, author of the *New Josephina*, and of the English Oratorian William Faber. This tradition has flourished in the twentieth century. In 1951, the Discalced Carmelites founded the Ibero-American Society of Josephology as well as began to publish the journal *Estudios Josefinos*. At the same time the North American Society of Josephology was founded in Montreal, and publication of the journal *Cahiers de Joséphologie* commenced. The centenary of the proclamation of St. Joseph as patron of the Universal Church was celebrated in Rome in 1970 with an international congress. The present exhibition of Spanish American Colonial images of St. Joseph at Saint Joseph's University in Philadelphia is to be situated in the context of these twentieth-century developments in the evolution of devotion to this beloved saint.

My colleagues Christopher Wilson, Joseph Chorpenning, and Barbara von Barghahn give a detailed account, in their analytical and interpretive essays, of various facets of St. Joseph's cult and iconography. This exhibition presents paintings from private collections in Virginia, Pennsylvania, Massachusetts, and Washington, D.C.—colonial paintings from the Schools of Mexico, Quito, and Cuzco. Some of these art works are attributed to Antonio Torres, Miguel Cabrera, and Manuel de Samaniego. They are evidence of how extensive in Spanish American Colonial society devotion to St. Joseph, the putative father of Christ who accompanies him almost like a guardian angel, was. From medieval times, the ordinary people loved this father protector for his simplicity and contemplated him with tenderness. This was the traditional image of St. Joseph of the Fathers of the Church, who regarded this saint as a "just man" on account of his prudence, silence, and humility before the mystery of the Incarnation.

This exhibition at Philadelphia's Jesuit university is apropos because one of the opportunities of this Quincentenary is to re-evaluate the images of Spanish American art, that is, iconography—in the present case, that of the patron of the University. This catalogue makes it clear how necessary a monograph about St. Joseph's iconography is. This is a project that has not even been realized in Valencia, the city whence I write, even though its world-renowned *Fallas* are celebrated on March 19th, the feast day of St. Joseph.

Santiago Sebastián López
Department of Art History
University of Valencia

January 25, 1992

Introduction

In the mid-nineteenth century Father William Faber, a priest of the Congregation of the Oratory in London, wrote this précis of the history of devotion to St. Joseph:

> Gerson was raised up to be its doctor and theologian, St. Teresa to be its saint, and St. Francis de Sales to be its popular leader and missioner. The houses of Carmel were like the Holy House of Nazareth to it, and the colleges of the Jesuits its peaceful sojourns in dark Egypt.[1]

This brief quotation aptly serves as a point of orientation for the exhibition "Patron Saint of the New World: Spanish American Colonial Images of Saint Joseph," for this catalogue that accompanies and provides commentary for this exhibition, and for the institution sponsoring these projects—Saint Joseph's University, the Jesuit university of Philadelphia.

For this exhibition of seventeenth-, eighteenth-, and nineteenth-century images of St. Joseph from Mexico, Peru, Ecuador, and Bolivia, the Jesuit university of Philadelphia offers a peaceful sojourn.[2] As the name of this University indicates, St. Joseph has always been a much beloved saint in the Society of Jesus, which has been pivotal in the development of devotion to the husband of the Virgin Mary and the guardian of Christ. Veneration of St. Joseph has been one of the hallmarks of the devotional life of the Society of Jesus from its origins. In the *Spiritual Exercises* St. Ignatius Loyola often introduced St. Joseph into the gospel meditations on the early life of our Lord; he also held St. Joseph up to his spiritual sons as an exemplar of paternal authority and filial obedience. Ignatius is said to have had an image of St. Joseph in his private oratory where he prayed, celebrated Mass, and commended to this saint all his concerns and difficulties.

After the Council of Trent, the Jesuits played a major role in promotion of devotion to St. Joseph. It is reported that in Spain, France, and the Netherlands all churches belonging to colleges of the Society were dedicated to St. Joseph. The Jesuits in Lyons were the first to build a church in St. Joseph's honor in France. Distinguished and highly influential Jesuit theologians such as St. Peter Canisius, Cornelius à Lapide, and Francisco Suárez diligently encouraged veneration of St. Joseph. After 1600 more than 130 works on St. Joseph were published by Jesuits. The invocation of St. Joseph as patron of the dying was largely due to the advocacy of the Jesuits.

The Jesuits carried their deep affection for St. Joseph with them to their missions in the Orient and in the New World. In South and North America they taught their spiritual children to revere and to imitate the reputed father of Jesus. When St. John de Breubeuf founded the first mission among the Hurons, he dedicated it to St. Joseph. The first Catholic church in Philadelphia was Old St. Joseph's, which was founded in 1733 by the Jesuit Joseph Greaton. It is at Old St. Joseph's Church where the roots of St. Joseph's University are to be found. St. Joseph was the baptismal patron of the first president of St. Joseph's University, Father Felix Joseph Barbelin, S.J., who cultivated a personal devotion to St. Joseph and who even composed a poem in his honor.

The present exhibition is a testimony to four hundred years of devotion of the Society of Jesus to St. Joseph as well as to this University's seriousness of purpose in reflecting on the identity and mission of its patron saint on the occasion of the quincentenary of the encounter of the New World. The essays in this catalogue aim to offer some assistance in this reflection, as we contemplate images of St. Joseph created in the New World. The first two essays focus on two saints and Doctors of the Church who are regarded as having a primary role in the evolution of devotion to St. Joseph in the early modern era: St. Teresa of Ávila and St. Francis de Sales. The way for these two saints' contribution was prepared by theologians during the Middle Ages, especially Jean Gerson, the great Chancellor of the Sorbonne and indefatigable promoter of St. Joseph's cult. Some of Gerson's most important ideas about Joseph are noted in the essays on Teresa and Francis.

Interestingly both Teresa and Francis were closely associated with the Society of Jesus. The arrival of the Jesuits in Ávila in the 1550s marked a turning point in Teresa's inner life as she began to consult them about her spiritual development. The first formal biography of Teresa, published in 1590, was written by the Jesuit Francisco de Ribera.[3] Francis de Sales was the great student of the Jesuits. At the Jesuit College of Clermont in Paris, he studied humanities and philosophy. When he went to study law at the University of Padua, Francis chose the Jesuit Antonio Possevino, an internationally renowned humanist and diplomat, to be his spiritual director. Francis often preached on St. Joseph at Jesuit colleges and churches, and seventeenth-century Jesuit writings on St. Joseph are in the tradition of Francis' devotional and affective method of reflecting on the husband of Mary and guardian of Christ.[4]

The first two essays have a twofold focus: first, how Teresa and Francis disseminated and promoted veneration of St. Joseph through their personal devotion, writings, and the religious communities they founded—the reformed Carmelites and the Visitation, respectively; and, second, how Teresa and Francis may have influenced the iconography of St. Joseph in Spanish American Colonial art. The third essay is an in-depth study of a specific aspect of St. Joseph's iconography: namely, how the image of the crowned figure of St. Joseph with his flowering staff, so ubiquitous in Spanish and in Spanish American Colonial art, evoked portraits of the Hapsburg kings, Incan legend about the foundation of the sacred city of Cuzco, and veneration of the sun by Aztec high priests.

The choice of the title of this exhibition is not capricious. Early in the Colonial period St. Joseph was declared the patron of New Spain, a vast territory that included present-day Mexico. "Thenceforth his feast was celebrated with great fervor and solemnity—and with the usual display of fireworks—everywhere in Spanish America."[5] In the seventeenth century it was revealed in a vision to Venerable Marie of the Incarnation, the Ursuline nun who was the first woman missionary to the New World, that "St. Joseph was the patron of the New World, and that it was owing to his intercession that she had been called to labour there in the salvation of souls."[6]

The distinguished Spanish art historian Santiago Sebastián López has pointed out that St. Joseph's role as patron of the New World accounts for the numerous images of him in Spanish American Colonial art.[7] Approximately half of the art works in the present exhibition depict events in the life of St. Joseph and the Holy Family such as the Marriage of Mary and Joseph, the Nativity of the Lord, the Flight into Egypt, the Return from Egypt, and the House of Nazareth. These events highlight Joseph as the person who struggles to be attentive and responsive to God's will in the circumstances of his state of life as husband and father and often in the midst of adversity—homelessness, persecution, residence in an alien and hostile country. The other half represent Joseph either lovingly holding the Christ Child in his arms or holding Jesus' hand and walking with him, casting into relief Joseph's role as earthly father, guardian, and protector of the Son of God. These images help us to appreciate better St. Joseph's invocation as patron of the Universal Church, families and family life, religious, workers, travelers, and the poor.

Without the assistance and cooperation of many people, this exhibition would not have become a reality. A special debt of gratitude is owed to Paul and Barbara Henkels for their generosity that made this exhibition possible; to the Art Museum of the Americas, Organization of American States, and to the private collectors for their graciousness in loaning us the art works for this exhibition; and to Rev. Nicholas S. Rashford, S.J., President of Saint Joseph's University, for his enthusiastic and unflagging support of this project from the start. Special thanks also go to Santiago Sebastián López for honoring this exhibition and St. Joseph's University by writing a preface to this catalogue; to Barbara von Barghahn and Christopher C. Wilson for their sage advice and invaluable assistance in putting this exhibition together, for serving as guest curators, and for contributing thoughtful and seminal essays to this catalogue; to Carmen Croce, director of Saint Joseph's University Press, and his talented staff for their customary outstanding work on the exhibition announcements, posters, and catalogue. Gratitude is also due to various offices and departments of Saint Joseph's University and to the fine people who manage and staff them for their help with various facets of the exhibition: Academic Affairs, Administrative Services, Alumni Relations, Development, Drexel Library, External Relations, Physical Plant, Security and Public Safety, Treasurer, and University Gallery (Boland Hall).

Joseph F. Chorpenning, O.S.F.S.

Feast of the Presentation of the Lord
February 2, 1992

Notes

1. Quoted in Susan T. Stein, *The Tapestry of St. Joseph: Chronological History of St. Joseph and His Apostle, Blessed Brother André* (Philadelphia: Apostle Publishing, 1991), p. 86.

2. The information in this and the next two paragraphs is based on the following sources: Anthony-Joseph Patrignani, S.J., *A Manual of Practical Devotion to St. Joseph*, translated and revised by a Member of the Society of Jesus (1865; Rockford, Illinois: Tan Books, 1982), pp. 59-60; Eleanor C. Donnelly, *A Memoir of Father Felix Joseph Barbelin, S.J.* (Philadelphia: Frank A. Fasy, 1886), pp. 259-62; Francis L. Filas, S.J., *The Man Nearest to Christ: Nature and Historic Development of the Devotion to St. Joseph* (Milwaukee: Bruce Publishing Company, 1944), pp. 156-59; and Joseph de Guibert, S.J., *The Jesuits: Their Spiritual Doctrine and Practice*, translated by William J. Young, S.J. (Chicago: Loyola University Press, 1964), pp. 389-90.

3. See James Brodrick, S.J., "St. Teresa and the Jesuits," in *St. Teresa of Ávila: Studies in Her Life, Doctrine, and Times*, edited by Fr. Thomas, O.C.D., and Fr. Gabriel, O.C.D. (Westminster, Maryland: Newman Press, 1963), pp. 222-35.

4. See Patrignani, p. 78; Roland Gauthier, C.S.C., "Saint Joseph dans l'histoire de la spiritualité," *Dictionnaire de Spiritualité*, vol. 8 (Paris: Beauchesne), cols. 1308-16, especially cols. 1311-12.

5. Filas, p. 158.

6. Patrignani, pp. 134-35.

7. Santiago Sebastián López, "Diffusion of Counter-Reformation Doctrine," in *Temples of Gold, Crowns of Silver: Reflections of Majesty in the Viceregal Americas*, edited by Barbara von Barghahn (Washington, D.C.: George Washington University, 1991), pp. 57-79, especially p. 71.

St. Teresa of Ávila's Holy Patron:
Teresian Sources for the Image of St. Joseph in Spanish American Colonial Art

Christopher Chadwick Wilson

The preeminence of the earthly father of Christ in art of the New World is, in large measure, a legacy of St. Teresa of Ávila (1515-82), the extraordinary mystical writer and reformer of the Carmelite order (Pl. 1).[1] The special veneration of St. Joseph by St. Teresa and her order in Spain inspired his popularity there and in the colonies, and shaped in significant ways his portrayal in Spanish American Colonial art. In her writings and through her reform, St. Teresa defined and extolled St. Joseph's attributes as a rescuer of souls in need, a patron of religious institutions, and a protector of travellers. Such qualities as these no doubt encouraged the religious orders to carry the image of St. Joseph on their mission to the New World.

PLATE 1. *Mother Teresa of Jesus, Foundress of the Discalced Carmelites*, Engraving from the 1588 edition of St. Teresa of Ávila's works, published in Madrid. This engraving, based on the 1576 portrait of St. Teresa painted by Fray Juan de la Miseria, must have introduced many inhabitants of Spain and the Americas to the image of the nun known in the Spanish-speaking world as Teresa of Jesus.

The Emergence in Spain of a "Glorious Patriarch"

Teresa's public devotion to the saint arose at a moment when veneration of Joseph was on the verge of blossoming. In the early fifteenth century, Jean Gerson (1362-1428), the Chancellor of the Sorbonne, wrote his fundamental text called the *Josephina*, a poem of 2957 verses extolling the virtues of the earthly father of Christ. Two important treatises were published in the first half of the sixteenth century: In 1522, the Dominican Isidore de Isolani published in Pavia his essay entitled *Summa of the Gifts of St. Joseph*. And in 1535, the first Spanish treatise on Joseph, a *Josephina* in the *Ascent of Mount Sion* by Bernardino de Laredo, a Franciscan, was published in Seville. The latter work contains twenty-six paragraphs in which the author described, with the aid of earlier writings of saints and doctors of the Church, the excellencies of St. Joseph.[2]

Despite the publication of these important texts, the art produced in Spain before the time of Teresa does not reveal a special interest in the figure of Joseph. Prior to the second half of the sixteenth century, Joseph was rarely depicted alone with the Christ Child. Gratiniano Nieto Gallo cites a late fifteenth-century panel by the Master of Perea as the only known example of a Spanish image produced before the sixteenth century in which Joseph appears isolated from a group.[3] Most often Joseph was portrayed as an old man, a wise and dignified observer of Christ and the Virgin rather than an active participant in the Holy Family.

There were, however, some representations of a younger and more energetic Joseph in early sixteenth-century Spanish painting, particularly in certain works by masters of the School of Valencia. The depiction of a more youthful Joseph may have resulted from Italian influence. In Raphael's *Marriage of the Virgin* of 1504, the Umbrian master portrayed the saint as a young man, probably in his early thirties. Fernando Yañez de Almedina returned to Valencia in 1506 after a sojourn in Italy, where he had studied the work of High Renaissance artists, especially Leonardo da Vinci. He painted a panel of *The Rest on the Flight into Egypt* for the Cathedral of Valencia, dated 1507-10, which features a Joseph of the same age as in the painting by Raphael, though of considerably stockier build.[4] Italian influence was again imported to Spain when Philip II brought in a team of painters for the decoration of the Palace-Monastery of the Escorial. Pellegrino Tibaldi (1527-96) and his assistants included images of a young and handsome Joseph for the frescoes of the Escorial's Lower Cloister (Pl. 2).[5] Nevertheless, only after the activity of Teresa and the diffusion of her writings did the depiction of a youthful Joseph, which already had taken root in sixteenth-century art, prevail in Spanish painting.

St. Joseph, Doctor of Heaven

PLATE 2.
Pellegrino Tibaldi, *The Flight Into Egypt*, ca. 1586. Lower Cloister, The Escorial Palace-Monastery.

Teresa's writings are replete with examples of how St. Joseph came to her rescue. Her earliest experience of Joseph's miraculous intercession centered around an illness which struck her as a young nun in the Carmelite convent of the Incarnation. Her story of how Joseph saved her from a crippling disease established him as a "doctor of heaven" who delivers a helpless soul from danger. She narrated this and her other experiences of the saint in the *Book of Her Life*, a fascinating account of her spiritual development through the year 1565, written under obedience for her confessors and spiritual directors. First published in 1588, this autobiography contains many events that later became subjects of Spanish American art of the Colonial period.

Teresa took the Carmelite habit in 1536 at the monastery of the Incarnation in Ávila, but she had a breakdown in health almost immediately after beginning her life in the monastery. She had gone through a period of illness prior to entering the Incarnation, but once within its walls, her maladies grew worse to include more frequent fainting spells and high fever. She experienced heart pains so severe "that it frightened any who witnessed them."[6] Since the doctors of Ávila could offer little help, her father sent her to the town of Becedas to be cured, but the harsh treatment there nearly killed her. In the summer of 1539 she returned to her father's house, where she suffered a paroxysm so severe that it left her in a coma for four days. After regaining consciousness, unable to move, Teresa insisted that she be taken back to the Incarnation, and thus "the one they expected to be brought back dead they received alive; but the body, worse than dead, was a pity to behold" (1:51).

Although she remained patient during this illness which kept her paralyzed for three years, at this point in her life Teresa desired to be well again, believing that if she were in good health she would be able to serve God better. Most of all, she wanted her health back so that she could remain alone in prayer. This was not possible in the infirmary of the Incarnation (1:51). It was with this motive, of seeking a cure so that she could be of more service to God, that she approached St. Joseph. She wrote:

> Since I saw myself so crippled and still so young and how helpless the doctors of earth were, I resolved to go for aid to the doctors of heaven that they might cure me.... I took for my advocate and lord the glorious St. Joseph and earnestly recommended myself to him. I saw clearly that as in this need so in other greater ones concerning honor and loss of soul this father and lord of mine came to my rescue in better ways than I knew how to ask for. I don't recall up to this day ever having petitioned him for anything that he failed to grant. It is an amazing thing the great many favors God has granted me through the mediation of this blessed saint, the dangers I was freed from both of body and soul.... For he being who he is brought it about that I could rise and walk and not be crippled (1:53-54).

Teresa adopted Joseph as a protector, calling him father and lord (1:53). It is important to note that during times of crisis her requests for divine assistance often took place before a holy image. Although we have no direct record of it, it seems likely that Teresa focused on the figure of Joseph in a painting or sculpture when she first took him as her patron, seeking his help. This would parallel a similar experience she had at the age of thirteen after the death of her mother:

> When I began to understand what I had lost, I went, afflicted, before an image of our Lady and besought her with many tears to be my mother. It seems to me that although I did this in simplicity it helped me. For I have found favor with this sovereign Virgin in everything I have asked of her, and in the end she has drawn me to herself (1:34).

Just as Teresa had begged the Virgin to be her mother in front of a statue, she must have requested that St. Joseph be her father by addressing him before an image, perhaps a narrative painting of the childhood of Christ at the Incarnation.

The role of images in Teresa's religious life is also illustrated by an experience in 1554, years after her illness, described by Teresa as a conversion which helped her to avoid occasions of falling into sin and to ascend to a higher level of prayer. This event occurred in the oratory of the Incarnation, where Teresa saw a statue of the wounded Christ, an *Ecce Homo*, that had been borrowed for the celebration of a feast. She described how she felt her heart break at beholding His great suffering, and she made the following request of Him:

> Beseeching Him to strengthen me once and for all that I might not offend Him, I threw myself down before Him with the greatest outpouring of tears. . . . I think I then said that I would not rise from there until he granted me what I was begging for. I believe certainly this was beneficial to me, because from that time on I went on improving (1:70-71).

This event, reaffirming the power of an image, must have strengthened further Teresa's wish to provide depictions of her father and lord St. Joseph in the monasteries of her reform. With his image available, the nuns would be inspired to beseech Joseph that they might obtain a beneficial response from him, as Teresa obtained favorable responses before the statue of the Virgin and the *Ecce Homo*.

Teresa emerged from the miraculous experience of Joseph's medical aid with "the desire to persuade all to be devoted to him" (1:54). Moreover, she believed that her cure was only one example of the many possibilities of Joseph's assistance. She held the conviction, from experience, that others should adopt him as a father, writing:

> For with other saints it seems the Lord has given them grace to be of help in one need, whereas with this glorious saint I have experience that he helps in all our needs and that the Lord wants us to understand that just as He was subject to St. Joseph on earth—for since bearing the title of father, being the Lord's tutor, Joseph could give the Child commands—so in heaven God does whatever he commands (1:53).

Through personal contacts with others, such as her relatives, the other nuns in the Incarnation, her confessors, and later in her life, benefactors and members of the Carmelite reform, she narrated her own experiences with the hope that they too would place themselves under Joseph's protection. She was successful in her persuasion. Teresa attested that the power of Joseph "has been observed by other persons, also through experience, whom I have told to recommend themselves to him. And so there are many who in experiencing this truth renew their devotion to him" (1:53-54).

Teresa concluded this section of the *Book of Her Life*, where she described Joseph's help during her illness, with the following piece of advice:

> I only ask for the love of God anyone who does not believe me to try, and he will see through experience the great good that comes from recommending oneself to this glorious patriarch and being devoted to him (1:54).

For Native Americans, the hundred years between 1550 and 1650 were a period of continuous epidemics and a disastrous decline in population. The diseases which arrived in the New World with the Spaniards, including smallpox, typhoid and measles, devastated the Indian civilizations.[7] No doubt St. Teresa's impassioned account of how St. Joseph, the "doctor of heaven," miraculously healed her paralysis had powerful reverberations in the Americas. In the midst of such rampant illness, the members of religious orders must have instructed the Indians concerning the curative powers of St. Joseph. This saint saved the Christ Child from Herod's massacre by leading the Holy Family into Egypt, and he rescued St. Teresa from being crippled when she sought his help.[8] In the wake of natural disasters, epidemics, and with the fresh memory of the violence done to their ancestors during the conquest, the Indians would have been moved by St. Teresa's advice to take Joseph as our father and protector since "in a powerful way he benefits souls who recommend themselves to him" (1:54).

THE CARPENTER OF NAZARETH:
BUILDER AND PROTECTOR OF A HOLY HOUSE

Teresa's eventful description of the founding of the monastery of St. Joseph, the first house of her Carmelite reform, set an important precedent for Joseph's patronage in the founding and preservation of religious institutions in Spain and the New World. The idea of founding a new monastery, where a small group of nuns could live like hermits, arose during a conversation at the Incarnation sometime in the late 1550s. Teresa's niece, a nun at the same monastery, suggested that a new Carmelite community be founded, where the nuns could lead a more austere and prayerful life than they could at the large monastery of the Incarnation.[9] Teresa sought to carry out this plan, and she intended that the monastery observe what she understood as the primitive Carmelite rule, with all its rigors, as opposed to the mitigated Carmelite rule observed at the Incarnation and all other Carmelite monasteries of the day.[10] The members of Teresa's reform were later called Discalced, meaning barefoot, Carmelites.

God immediately made it clear to Teresa that the proposed religious house would have the great favor of St. Joseph's patronage. She wrote:

> One day after Communion, His Majesty earnestly commanded me to strive for this new monastery with all my powers, and He made great promises that it would be founded and that He would be greatly served in it. He said it should be called St. Joseph and that this saint would keep watch over us at one door, and our Lady at the other, that Christ would remain with us, and that it would be a star shining with great splendor (1:217).

Teresa had to overcome severe obstacles in founding the monastery, not the least of which was purchasing and renovating an appropriate house when she had scarce material resources. She affirmed that the intervention of St. Joseph protected the difficult project. Teresa wrote that on one occasion she needed to hire some workmen to prepare the house, but she had no means available to pay them. Subsequently,

> St. Joseph, my true father and lord, appeared to me and revealed to me that I would not be lacking, that I should hire them. And so I did, without so much as a penny, and the Lord in ways that amazed those who heard about it provided for me (1:225).

Interestingly, the lacking funds which finally did arrive, thus fulfilling St. Joseph's promise, came from the New World. Teresa's brother Lorenzo (1519-1580), who was living at the time in Quito, Ecuador, sent the money to Teresa himself. Teresa's written response to Lorenzo must be considered one of the first instances of the transmission of her devotion to Joseph to the New World. In a letter dated December 23, 1561, she wrote:

> I have bought the house, keeping the purchase secret, but I can find no way of getting the necessary work done on it. However, as God wants it done, He will provide for me, so I have put all my trust in Him and am engaging the workmen. It seemed a foolish thing to do—but now His Majesty comes and moves you to provide the money; and what amazed me most was that you added those forty pesos, of which I had the greatest need. I think St. Joseph, whose name the house is to bear, was not going to let me want for them: I know he will repay you.[11]

On August 15 of the same year, still proceeding with challenging preparations for the new monastery, Teresa experienced a powerful rapture. She saw herself being clothed in a brilliant white robe. At first she did not see who was putting the shining vestment on her, but

> Afterward I saw our Lady at my right side and my father St. Joseph at the left, for they were putting that robe on me. I was given to understand that I was now cleansed of my sins. After being clothed and while experiencing the most marvelous delight and glory, it seemed to me then that our Lady took me by the hands. She told me I made her very happy in serving the glorious St. Joseph, that I should believe that what I was striving for in regard to this monastery would be accomplished, that the Lord and those two would be greatly served in it, that I shouldn't fear there would ever be any failure in this matter . . . because they would watch over us (1:226).

During the course of this project, Teresa faced intense opposition from ecclesiastical authorities, from the city, and especially from within the community of the Incarnation. Some of the other nuns there resented her intention to found a more enclosed monastery so much that, Teresa wrote, "several of them said I should be thrown into the prison cell" (1:220).

Nevertheless, Teresa continued to follow the divine command to found a monastery named for the earthly father of Christ. In 1562, while putting the finishing touches on the building, Teresa placed a painting of Joseph over the altar of the church, since he was patron of the foundation. Also remembering the promise the Lord had made to her about Joseph keeping watch over the door, she placed a statue of the saint over the entrance to the church. He was "adorned with a vestment and hat in hand, of silk, and his flowering rod."[12] On August 24, 1562, the monastery of St. Joseph was founded. On this day, Teresa felt a consolation in having established "another church in this city, dedicated to my glorious father St. Joseph, in whose honor none was yet built" (1:242).

Teresa envisioned the monastery as having an important role which she revealed in the *Way of Perfection*, probably written in 1566 as a response to her nuns' urging that she present them with a book about prayer. In the opening chapter of this book she explained that she founded St. Joseph's in Ávila with such strict observance of poverty and external austerity because news had reached her of the turmoil "the Lutherans had caused and how much this miserable sect was growing" (2:41). She felt that in the prayerful atmosphere of St. Joseph's the nuns could do everything in their power to prevent the devil from carrying away one more soul. Teresa intended for the monastic community to "be occupied in prayer for those who are the defenders of the Church and for preachers and for learned men who protect her from attack" (2:42). She approached this assignment with the same zeal and sense of purpose as a militant defender of the faith, and she urged her nuns to pray with a similar determination:

> O my sisters in Christ, help me beg these things of the Lord. This is why He has gathered you together here. This is your vocation. These must be the business matters you are engaged in (2:42).

Teresa's account of the founding of St. Joseph's must have resounded with a special significance in the colonies because her story was of a religious house founded to combat heresy, to win souls to Christ. In the New World, the religious orders were faced with the tremendous task of converting an entire indigenous population, totally unschooled in the Christian faith, to Catholicism. Not surprisingly, the protection of St. Joseph, the patron of Teresa's effort to defend the Church, was sought by the religious orders in the Americas.

A Father to Many Foundations

Teresa was deeply interested in the New World, both in its exploration and in its inhabitants. Seven of her brothers, members of her own family, went on expeditions to the colonies, and she herself had an ardent desire to save souls there.[13] Even though Teresa was never able to join the members of other religious orders embarking on their missions to the Spanish colonies, she held the firm belief that lost souls could be brought to Christ through prayer. In fact, her concern for the spiritual salvation of Native Americans increased her work of reform. A letter to her brother Lorenzo in Quito, dated January 17, 1570, reflects her apprehensions about the state of the indigenous population of the Americas:

> What grieves me so much is to see so many souls being lost, and the thought of those Indians causes me no small distress. May the Lord give them light, for both here and in the Indies there is sore misery.[14]

In the *Book of Her Foundations*, Teresa's adventurous story of founding monasteries throughout Spain, she wrote of an experience that gave new momentum to her Carmelite reform. In 1566 a Franciscan missionary, just returned from Mexico, visited the monastery of St. Joseph's in Ávila. Through the locutorio grille he spoke to Teresa of the "many millions of souls that were being lost there for want of Christian instruction" (3:101). After hearing this

PLATE 3.
El Greco, *Preliminary Sketch for St. Joseph and the Christ Child*, ca. 1597. Sacristy, Toledo Cathedral.

account, Teresa begged Christ to help her win some souls to His service. He gave her the reply, "Wait a little, daughter, and you will see great things" (3:102).

Teresa went on to found sixteen more monasteries in Spain, in addition to St. Joseph's in Ávila. Twelve of her foundations were named for St. Joseph. She also initiated a branch of the Discalced Carmelites for friars. Teresa must have felt that the prayers of the sisters and friars within the reformed order would contribute to the effort of evangelization in the New World. She must have also known that as the order continued to expand it would someday travel to the Spanish colonies.

On numerous occasions Teresa furnished her monasteries with images of Joseph. In 1571, for example, in a letter to Don Alonso Ramírez, one of the patrons of the Discalced Carmelite nuns in Toledo, she wrote: "Tell Señor Diego Ortiz that I beg him not to forget to put a statue of my lord St. Joseph over the church door."[15] As Teresa multiplied the number of Discalced Carmelite foundations, she set an important pattern of including depictions of Joseph in religious houses. This pattern was followed in the New World, resulting in many Native Americans coming into contact with Joseph's paternal image. In this way, some of the Indians, for whose salvation Teresa had prayed, came to know of St. Joseph as a direct result of her veneration of him.

Teresa's devotion to Joseph spread well beyond the walls of her monasteries into Spanish religious life and ultimately to the New World. Within her own order, the popularity of Joseph continued to flourish after her death in 1582. In 1590 Joseph was named patron of the Carmelite reform in Spain.[16] In the year 1591, the combined number of foundations of Discalced Carmelite friars and nuns stood at eighty-one, attesting to the remarkable growth of the order. By this date the reform had spread to Portugal, Italy, Africa, and Mexico, carrying with it the paternal image of St. Joseph.[17]

PLATE 4.
Francisco de Zurbarán, *St. Joseph Walking with the Christ Child*, ca. 1636. Saint-Medard, Paris.

The Discalced Carmelite friar Jerónimo Gracián de la Madre de Dios (1545-1614) played a key role in helping to propagate devotion to St. Joseph. Gracián joined St. Teresa's reform in 1572 and subsequently developed a very close relationship with the Mother Foundress. Following Teresa's initiative, he wrote *Josephina. Summary of the Excellencies of Glorious Saint Joseph, Husband of the Virgin Mary*. This work, first published in 1597 and subsequently reprinted in many editions, became one of the most well-known pieces of writing on St. Joseph. Gracián synthesized earlier authors' words about Joseph, and he also related examples of Teresa's veneration of the saint. Cited in Francisco Pacheco's *Art of Painting* of 1649, Gracián's book made important contributions to Joseph's iconography.[18]

Among other things, Gracián defended the depiction of the young Joseph, explaining that although St. Epiphanius, a Father of the Church, claimed Joseph to be eighty years old at the time of his marriage to the Virgin, the majority of authors said he must have been between forty and fifty years old. The proof of this age is that Joseph was selected to sustain the Virgin with the work of his hands, to travel with her and to defend her.[19] Gracián also wrote that St. Joseph was the man who most resembled Christ and the Virgin "in countenance, speech, physical constitution, customs, inclinations, and manner."[20] This description must have contributed to the manner in which Joseph was portrayed in Spanish and Spanish American Colonial art with features similar to those of the adult Christ. Gracián emphasized the beautiful image of Joseph holding the Christ Child, writing that when the saint "entered the city with the Child in his arms, all of heaven became a window, the angels admiring to see God in the arms of a carpenter."[21]

Influenced by the Carmelites, other religious orders in Spain renewed their veneration of Joseph and helped to extend his popularity, particularly the Franciscans and the Jesuits. The increased honor given to the saint resulted in an abundance of Golden-Age paintings depicting Joseph alone with the Christ Child. The new devotion to Joseph favored the image of the saint as a strong, youthful man, as he had been depicted in the cloister frescoes at the Escorial. A.L. Mayer observed that El Greco, in the high altar of the Chapel of St. Joseph in Toledo of 1597-99, was one of the first artists to glorify the figure of St. Joseph in response to the increased veneration given to him (Pl. 3).[22] El Greco represented the earthly father of Christ as a handsome man in his early thirties, standing with his arm placed protectively around the Christ Child's shoulder. He guards the Child with the same fatherly assurance that Teresa promised he would guard the soul seeking his assistance.

Teresa's description of Joseph as a powerful protector must have been strengthened further by Johannus Molanus's work *On the History of Sacred Images*, first published in 1570 and reprinted many times until the eighteenth century. This treatise, cited by Pacheco and influential on Spanish artists, described Joseph as a young and strong man. Molanus advised that the Christ Child be painted at the hand of Joseph, since this portrayal shows that Christ was submissive to his earthly father.[23]

The portrayal of the handsome St. Joseph, walking with the Christ Child in a landscape, grew in popularity during the seventeenth century. In the 1630s Francisco de Zurbarán (1598-1664) painted his beautiful rendition of the subject for the Monastery of Discalced Mercedarians in Seville, for the high altar of their church which was dedicated to St. Joseph (Pl. 4).[24] The depiction of Joseph embracing his son was also prevalent. Bartolomé Esteban Murillo (1617-1682) painted several devotional works of a half-length figure of St. Joseph, holding the Christ Child close to his chest, as in the work in St. Louis, 1670-75 (Pl. 5). Variations on these two types of portrayals of the saint became extremely popular in the Spanish colonies.

PLATE 5. Bartolomé Esteban Murillo, *St. Joseph with the Christ Child*, 1670-75. Washington University, St. Louis.

THE VOYAGE TO THE NEW WORLD

St. Joseph played another important role for Teresa: he was a protector on her many journeys to found monasteries. Teresa travelled with her nuns by carriage, covered wagon or on muleback. She and her companions recorded many experiences of the challenges they faced together: poor roads, extreme heat, floods, and sometimes a scarcity of food and water (Pl. 6). In the face of such difficulties, Teresa was always able to turn for help to her father and lord, St. Joseph. In describing the foundress' devotion to Joseph, Gracián wrote in his *Josephina* that "on all of her foundations she carried with her a statue of this glorious saint."[25]

When Teresa and her nuns were travelling through the Sierra Morena in 1574 on the way to the foundation in Beas de Segura, they lost the way in a dangerous place among high cliffs. Teresa, seeing that it was impossible to go forwards or backwards, commanded the nuns to pray to God and to St. Joseph. Then they saw an old man, standing in a ravine, who shouted to them the warning that if they went any farther they would fall and perish. The men who were travelling with them, priests and secular persons, asked the man which way they should go. He responded that the carriages would not be able to pass by one route they had before them, and then, miraculously, the lost group found another path, free of all the previous danger. Some members of the party wanted to go back to search for that man who had given them the way. St. Teresa responded that this would be of no use, that the man who freed them from danger was her father St. Joseph, and that no one would find him.[26]

PLATE 6. Juan Correa (Mexico), *St. Teresa as Pilgrim*, ca. 1690-1700. Museo Regional del Carmen, Mexico San Angel, D.F. (Elisa Vargas Lugo).

PLATE 7.
School of Cuzco (Peru), *Allegorical Flotilla of Salvation*, ca. 1650-80. Collection Guillermo Boza Vega León, Lima.

When travelling across the sea from Spain to the New World, on their way to spread the order founded by Teresa, the Discalced Carmelites must have carried with them images of Joseph, a protector for their journey, just as the Mother Foundress had carried a statue of him with her on all her journeys to new foundations. The Discalced Carmelite friars first brought the reform to the New World when they made a foundation in Mexico City in 1586.[27] In 1602, the Discalced Carmelite nuns established their first American convent in Mexico at Puebla de los Angeles. During the seventeenth century the friars were confined primarily to Mexico, but communities of Discalced Carmelite nuns, striving to follow the Teresian ideal, were founded in such cities as Bogotá (1606) in Colombia, Quito (1653) and Cuenca (1682) in Ecuador, Sucre (1665) and Potosí (1687) in Bolivia, and Lima (1643), Cuzco (1673) and Ayacucho (1683) in Peru.[28]

Teresa was beatified by Paul V in 1614 and canonized by Gregory XV in 1622. While Teresa's popularity grew during the seventeenth century, and as the miraculous favors which Joseph performed for her on her journeys and during the foundations of her monasteries became even more widely known, members of other religious orders must have invoked this saint for his protection as they sailed across the ocean to spread the Catholic faith.

A good example of Joseph's patronage may be seen in a seventeenth-century painting from the Cuzco School of Peru, entitled *The Allegorical Flotilla of Salvation* (Pl. 7). In the sky, overseeing the entire enterprise of the sea journey, is the figure of St. Joseph embracing the Christ Child. He is the patron and protector of this important voyage, both the allegorical voyage of the Catholic Church, with its members, to the port of salvation, and also the voyage of Christianity to a new land.

The painting also depicts three ships, each containing a radiant passenger: St. Teresa of Ávila on the far left, the Crucified Christ in the middle, and the Virgin with the Christ Child on the right. Beneath the ships, two figures, identified by Barbara von Barghahn as Inca natives, hold a banner bearing the Latin phrase *Navis Intitoris de Longe Portans Panem*—"The Ships Which Travel from a Long Distance Carry Bread."[29] The depiction of Teresa on the ship implies the many journeys which the foundress mystically made to the New World as her books were carried across the sea and as her reform was nurtured in the Spanish Colonies.

PLATE 8.
José Avitavilli, *St. Joseph Walking with the Christ Child and St. Catherine of Alexandria*, ca. 1597. Conventa de la Recoleta, Cuzco (Santiago Sebastián López).

Barbara von Barghahn has observed that the predominance of travel during the Colonial period—voyages back and forth from Europe to the New World, travel within the colonies to major centers and also to more remote regions for the purpose of evangelization—must have contributed to the popularity of the subjects of *The Flight Into Egypt* and *The Rest on the Flight into Egypt* (Catalogue 9, 13).[30] In these images, Joseph appears as the strong guardian of the Holy Family, protecting them on their passages to other lands, just as he also protected Teresa and her nuns on their travels.

THE IMAGE OF ST. JOSEPH IN THE NEW WORLD

During the Colonial period, art was needed in the New World for the decoration of the new monasteries and churches which administered the Catholic faith to the entire population, including: the Indians, who had to be instructed, through images, about the personages of Christianity; the *mestizos*, individuals of Indian and Spanish parentage; and the *criollos*, Spaniards born in the New World. The late sixteenth and the seventeenth century was a time of monumental construction of religious edifices in the New World. One observer, a Carmelite friar who travelled through Mexico, Central America and Peru between the years 1610 and 1620, reported that Mexico City alone contained sixteen convents of nuns.[31] With the growth of the Church in the New World, the number of ecclesiastics living in the colonies soared. In 1611, the population of Lima was reported to be 26,500, and a census calculated that ten percent of the population were priests, canons, friars and nuns.³² Moreover, this rise in church and monastery construction was not limited to the major Colonial cities. With the aim of instructing the Indians, the religious orders ventured into the outlying areas, constructing churches in some very remote regions. Luis Enrique Tord cites a group of sixteen churches, built from the fifteenth to nineteenth centuries in the valley of Collaguas, north of Arequipa, in a place so isolated that they were forgotten until the 1980s.³³

PLATE 9. Bartolomé Esteban Murillo, *St. Joseph Walking with the Christ Child*, ca. 1670. Monastery of the Discalced Franciscans, Lima (Jorge Bernales Ballesteros).

This period was also the time when devotion to Joseph flowered in Spain and in the colonies. Teresa's written accounts of St. Joseph's miraculous patronage of her monasteries must have encouraged the founders of the newly constructed religious edifices in the New World to include images of the holy patriarch in their buildings. Two important parts of Teresa's story of the founding of St. Joseph's in Ávila should be remembered: first, with Joseph's assistance, she successfully overcame difficult obstacles to establish the monastery; and, second, under Joseph's patronage, the house was founded to fight heresy and to assist the defenders of the church. Gracián, in his *Josephina*, wrote: "and as the glorious St. Joseph was a builder and collaborated with Jesus Christ and His Mother on the foundation of the Catholic Church, so the rest of the foundations of all the monasteries in the spiritual structure, in particular structures of edifices, he has favored miraculously."³⁴ As an example of the miraculous patronage of St. Joseph, Gracián then narrated the story of Joseph telling Teresa to hire the workmen even though she had no money, and of how he promised her that she would not be lacking.³⁵

The religious institutions in the colonies, in their effort to establish the Catholic faith in the New World, had another important reason to include the image of Joseph in their buildings: St. Joseph was viewed as the first saint of the New Law ushered in by the coming of Christ. Gracián wrote:

> St. Joseph was the first Christian of the world. . . . Even though the ancients saved themselves by their faith in the Messiah, they were not called Christians but Israelites, but St. Joseph was the first who, after the Virgin Mary, knew and adored Christ incarnate.³⁶

St. Joseph's role as the first Christian gave his image a special value as the Church worked to convert an entire indigenous population to the faith.

PLATE 10. Diego Quispe Tito (Peru), *St. Joseph with the Christ Child*, ca. 1630-40. Frank Barrows Freyer Collection, The Denver Art Museum, 1969.354.

The development of the portrayal of Joseph in the Andean region of South America will serve to illustrate the importance of his image for the propagation of the faith.³⁷ At first, to help meet the demand for religious images, European art works and artists were imported to South America. In 1575, an expedition of Jesuits arrived in Peru. Among this group was Bernardo Bitti, a painter formed by Italian Mannerism, who was to become the greatest artist working in South America during the sixteenth century.³⁸ Bitti's close pupil was José Avitavilli, also an Italian Jesuit, who arrived in Peru in the early 1590s.³⁹ Avitavilli painted a *St. Joseph Walking with the Christ Child* for the Convento de la Recoleta in Cuzco (Pl. 8). The work is thought to be a copy of an earlier composition which Bitti painted in the year 1595 for the College of the Society of Jesus in the same city, following the request of the Jesuit Manuel Vázquez.⁴⁰ Bitti's original painting, nearly contemporaneous with El Greco's work for the Chapel of St. Joseph in Toledo, must have been one of the earliest images produced in the colonies of the venerated Joseph leading the Christ Child by the hand. In Avitavilli's version of Bitti's work, the sturdy figure of Joseph seems closely related to the robust St. Joseph type painted by the Italian Mannerist Pellegrino Tibaldi at the cloister of the Escorial. This similarity in monumental form is explainable by the fact that both Tibaldi and Bitti were deeply influenced by the art of Michelangelo.⁴¹

PLATE 11.
Anton Wierix, *St. Joseph with the Christ Child*, ca. 1600, copper engraving. (John B. Knipping).

Avitavilli's composition includes the head of a female figure at the bottom of the canvas, identified by José de Mesa and Teresa Gisbert as St. Catherine of Alexandria.[42] This third-century noblewoman underwent a mystical marriage to Christ and dedicated herself to preaching the Christian faith. She converted an entire group of philosophers selected by the pagan Emperor Maximum II to refute her teaching. Catherine was finally martyred under Maximum's persecution, but only after she had successfully converted the emperor's wife and her entire retinue.[43] St. Catherine was an excellent iconographic model of discipleship, committed to the propagation of Christianity. Her inclusion with St. Joseph, the protector of a religious house and community, implies the alliance of earthly defense of the faith with Joseph's assistance from heaven.

Paintings by Spanish masters were also shipped to the colonies. During the seventeenth century, works by El Greco, Pacheco and Zurbarán arrived in Peru.[44] Diego Ángulo Iñíguez has accepted a *St. Joseph Walking with the Child Jesus*, in the Monastery of Discalced Franciscans in Lima, as a work of Murillo (Pl. 9).[45] Many copies were made of this particular painting, contributing to the subject's popularity in the Andean region.[46]

With the economic decline of Spain, there was a sharp decrease in the number of Italian, Flemish and even Spanish artists arriving in South America during the seventeenth century.[47] By the 1680s, as local schools of painting began to develop, particularly in the centers of Cuzco in Peru, Potosí in present-day Bolivia, and Quito in Ecuador, the artists were usually Indians or mestizos. A popular style of painting emerged which blended the indigenous artistic traditions of the Indians with the Christian iconography brought from Europe.[48] An eighteenth-century *St. Joseph Walking with the Christ Child* by an artist of the Cuzco School follows the iconography of the painting by Murillo in Lima, yet it reveals that the European Baroque tendency towards naturalism, correct anatomy and perspective was less important than the creation of brilliantly colored, monumental figures strolling through a beautiful landscape suggestive of paradise (Catalogue 11).[49]

PLATE 12.
Otto Venius, *Anne of St. Bartholomew*, 1620. Monastery of the Discalced Carmelites, Antwerp.

Another popular motif were the half-length compositions of Joseph holding the child. A magnificent example of this subject was painted in the second half of the seventeenth century by Diego Quispe Tito (1611-1681), an Indian master who worked in Peru and signed himself "inga," referring to his indigenous Andean heritage (Pl. 10).[50] Joseph holds a lily, a reference to the saint's chastity. Lilies also appear in the border. This work's particularly abundant blooms, filled with yellow pistils, may reflect Joseph's role as nurturer, both of the Christ Child and of the helpless soul in need of protection.

In the New World, the paternal image of Joseph holding the infant Christ must have first arisen from Flemish engravings, and been reinforced by the devotional paintings of Murillo and his workshop. Many books, including lives of the saints, came to the New World from the Plantin/Moretus Press in Antwerp which operated in the service of the Spanish monarchs. The engravings in these books, by artists such as Collaert, Galle and Wierix, served as sources for painters working in the Americas.[51] Anton Wierix the Younger produced a copper engraving of *St. Joseph with the Christ Child* that must have been used in the colonies by artists such as Diego Quispe Tito (Pl. 11).

The presence of Joseph in Flemish engravings must have increased as the saint's popularity grew in this region of Europe. Two of the nuns closest to Teresa of Ávila, Anne of Jesus and Anne of St. Bartholomew, played important roles in propagating devotion to Joseph in France and the Low Countries. Anne of Jesus (1545-1621) founded Discalced Carmelite monasteries in Paris (1604), Pontoise and Dijon (1605), as well as Brussels, Louvain and Mons (1607-08).[52] Anne of St. Bartholomew (1549-1626) founded monasteries in Tours (1608) and in

Antwerp (1612), where she remained until her death (Pl. 12).⁵³ The regents of the Spanish Netherlands, Isabel Clara Eugenia, daughter of Philip II, and Albert of Austria, venerated Anne of St. Bartholomew as a living saint. This Spanish nun had served as Teresa's secretary and nurse, and because of her closeness to the Mother Foundress, her advice was sought in both spiritual and political matters. When Anne established the Discalced Carmelite foundation in Antwerp, Isabel Clara Eugenia laid the foundation stone.⁵⁴ Therefore, bearing in mind the friendship between Isabel and Anne, it is interesting to note that Jan Galle dedicated to the Archduchess a series of prints, partly designed by Wierix, entitled *Life of St. Joseph*.⁵⁵ Like Teresa and her spiritual daughters, Isabel too was especially devoted to the earthly father of Christ.

PLATE 13. Gaspar Miguel de Berrío (Bolivia), *Patronage of St. Joseph*, 1737. Museo de la Moneda, Potosí, Bolivia (Teresa Gisbert).

In 1679 Pope Innocent XI, at the request of the regents and groups of devotees, declared the Southern Netherlands to be under the protection of St. Joseph.⁵⁶ The flourishing veneration of Joseph undoubtedly made his image more frequent and more devotional in Flemish engravings, thus contributing to the saint's predominance in art of the New World.

ST. JOSEPH, FATHER AND PROTECTOR FOR ALL HUMANKIND

St. Joseph remained a favorite subject of Andean painting throughout the Colonial period. During the eighteenth century, especially, he was portrayed with extraordinary authority and majesty. A painting dated 1737 by Gaspar Miguel de Berrío, a master of the School of Potosí, depicts a regal figure of Joseph, clothed in a resplendent gold-adorned fabric, holding a scepter and wearing a crown like that of a king (Pl. 13). His gigantic cloak is outstretched by angels to shelter a large group of ecclesiastical figures, including the four evangelists, the four Latin Fathers of the Church, and St. Teresa of Ávila, who holds an open book and a pen. The Heavenly Trinity sits in the sky, presiding over this glorification of the husband of Mary, the guardian of Christ, and the holy patron who is always providing his assistance. Here the viewer witnesses the status Joseph has achieved in Colonial society. He is depicted as a king whose patronage extends not only to individual souls and religious communities, but to the entire Church. St. Joseph, Teresa's lord and father, has become patron of the Church, offering his loving protection to all humankind.

Notes

1. This essay is dedicated to the memory of Kitty L. Davy (1891-1991), with heartfelt appreciation for her determination to walk always in the way of perfection. Much of the material in this essay is drawn from my M.A. Thesis of the same title, The George Washington University, 1992.

2. For a concise summary of the development of devotion to St. Joseph in the history of Christian spirituality, see Roland Gauthier, C.S.C., "St. Joseph dans l'histoire de la spiritualité," *Dictionnaire de Spiritualité*, vol. 8 (Paris: Beauchesne, 1974), cols. 1308-16.

3. Gratiniano Nieto Gallo, "San José en el arte español," *Estudios Josefinos*, 2 (1947), 224.

4. For information on Yañez, see Chandler Rathfon Post, *The Valencian School in the Early Renaissance* (Cambridge: Harvard University Press, 1953), pp. 175-276.

5. For a discussion of the decoration of the Lower Cloister of the Escorial, see Barbara von Barghahn, *Age of Gold, Age of Iron: Renaissance Spain and Symbols of Monarchy* (Lanham, Maryland: University Press of America, 1985), pp. 78-84.

6. See *The Collected Works of St. Teresa of Ávila, I: The Book of Her Life, Spiritual Testimonies, Soliloquies; II: The Way of Perfection, Meditations on the Song of Songs, The Interior Castle; III: The Book of Her Foundations, Minor Works*, translated by Kieran Kavanaugh, O.C.D., and Otilio Rodríguez, O.C.D. (Washington: Institute of Carmelite Studies Publications, 1976-85), 1:42. All subsequent references and quotations from St. Teresa's books are taken from this translation and are indicated by volume and page number.

7. Charles Gibson, *Spain in America* (New York: Harper & Row, 1966), p. 141.

8. Matthew 2.14.

9. E. Allison Peers, *A Handbook to the Life and Times of St. Teresa and St. John of the Cross* (London: Burnes and Oates, 1954), p. 7.

10. Teresa wrote, "We observe the rule of our Lady of Mt. Carmel and keep it without mitigation as ordained by the Friar Cardinal Hugo of Saint Sabina and given in 1248, in the fifth year of the pontificate of Pope Innocent IV" (1:250). The mitigated rule to which Teresa refers resulted from the Bull of Mitigation published in 1432 by Eugenius IV. See Peers, *Handbook*, p. 7.

11. See Letter 2 in *The Letters of St. Teresa of Jesus*, translated by E. Allison Peers, 2 vols. (1951; London: Sheed and Ward, 1980), 1:30.

12. Jerónimo de San José, *Historia del Carmen Descalzo*, vol. 1, IV (Madrid, 1637), p. 705, quoted in P. Fortunato de Jesús Sacramentado, O.C.D., "Santa Teresa de Jesús y su espíritu josefino," *Estudios Josefinos*, 13 (1953), 35.

13. For the dates of Teresa's brothers' departures for the New World, see "A Teresian Chronology" in *The Collected Works of St. Teresa of Ávila*, 3: 83-91.

14. See Letter 19 in *Letters of St. Teresa of Jesus*, 1: 75.

15. See Letter 24 in *Letters of St. Teresa of Jesus*, 1: 84.

16. Gauthier, col. 1312.

17. Peers, *Handbook*, p. 99.

18. See Francisco Pacheco, *Arte de la pintura*, 2 vols. (Madrid: Instituto de Valencia de Don Juan, 1956). Pacheco cites Gracián in 1:305 and in 2:231, 235, 238, 240, 253, 255, 259, 264, 267.

19. Jerónimo Gracián de la Madre de Dios, *Josefina. Summario de las excelencias del glorioso S. Joseph, esposo de la Virgen María*, in *Obras de Jerónimo Gracián de la Madre de Dios*, edited by Silverio de Santa Teresa, 3 vols. (Burgos: El Monte Carmelo, 1933), 2:387.

20. Gracián, p. 481.

21. Gracián, p. 387.

22. A.L. Mayer, "Notas sobre la iconografía sagrada en las obras del Greco," *Archivo español de arte*, 43 (1941), 164.

23. Mayer, p. 165.

24. Jeanine Baticle, *Zurbarán* (New York: Metropolitan Museum of Art, 1987), pp. 149-52.

25. Gracián, p. 476.

26. Gracián, p. 477.

27. Peers, *Handbook*, p. 268.

28. For a history of the Discalced Carmelites in Latin America, see Alberto de la Virgen del Carmen, *Historia de la reforma teresiana (1562-1962)* (Madrid: Editorial de Espiritualidad, 1968), pp. 537-47.

29. Barbara von Barghahn, "Imaging the Cosmic Goddess: Sacred Legends and Metaphors for Majesty," in *Temples of Gold, Crowns of Silver: Reflections of Majesty in the Viceregal Americas*, edited by Barbara von Barghahn (Washington D.C.: George Washington University, 1991), p. 103.

30. Barbara von Barghahn, "Guardians from a Citadel of Light: Mirrors of Virtue for the Earthly Pilgrim," in *Temples of Gold, Crowns of Silver: Reflections of Majesty in the Viceregal Americas. Exhibition Guide* (Washington D.C.: George Washington University, 1991).

31. Antonio Vázquez de Espinosa, *Compendium and Description of the Indies, c. 1620*, translated by Charles Upson Clark (Washington, D.C.: Smithsonian Institution Press, 1942), pp. 157-59, 161-62, quoted in *Cross and Sword: An Eyewitness Account of Christianity in Latin America*, edited by H. McKennie Goodpasture (Maryknoll, N.Y.: Orbis, 1989), pp. 42-43.

32. Clarence Haring, "The Wealth of the Church," in *The Roman Catholic Church in Colonial Latin America*, edited by Richard E. Greenleaf (New York: Knopf, 1971) p. 178, quoted in Goodpasture, pp. 43-44.

33. Luis Enrique Tord, "The Viceroyalty of Peru, 1532-1825," in *Gloria in Excelsis: The Virgin and Angels in Viceregal Painting of Peru and Bolivia*, edited by Barbara Duncan (New York: Center for Inter-American Relations, 1986), p. 15.

34. Gracián, p. 476.

35. Gracián, p. 476.

36. Gracián, p. 479.

37. For a discussion of the iconography of St. Joseph in Latin American Colonial art, see Santiago Sebastián López, *El barroco iberoamericano* (Madrid: Ediciones Encuentro, 1990), pp. 199-217.

38. For an investigation of Bernardo Bitti and his collaborators and disciples, see José de Mesa and Teresa Gisbert, *Historia de la pintura cuzqueña,* vol. 1 (Lima: Banco Wiese, 1982), pp. 56-68.

39. Mesa and Gisbert, *Historia,* p. 66.

40. Mesa and Gisbert, *Historia,* pp. 62, 66.

41. See Arnold Hauser, *Mannerism: The Crisis of the Renaissance and the Origin of Modern Art* (Cambridge: Harvard University Press, 1965), p. 156, and Mesa and Gisbert, *Historia,* pp. 56-57.

42. Mesa and Gisbert, *Historia,* p. 66.

43. George Ferguson, *Signs and Symbols in Christian Art* (New York: Oxford University Press, 1961), pp. 110-11.

44. Teresa Gisbert, "Andean Painting," in *Gloria in Excelsis: The Virgin and Angels in Viceregal Painting of Peru and Bolivia,* p. 25.

45. Diego Ángulo Iñíguez, *Murillo: Catálogo crítico,* vol. 2 (Madrid: Espasa-Calpe, 1981), pp. 262-63. Jorge Bernales Ballesteros, however, considered this painting to be a workshop copy of Murillo's composition of the same subject, now at the Hermitage Leningrad. See Jorge Bernales Ballesteros, "La pintura en Lima durante el virreinato," *Pintura en el virreinato del Perú* (Lima: Banco Crédito del Perú, 1989), pp. 88-90.

46. Mesa and Gisbert, *Historia,* p. 117.

47. Gisbert, "Andean Painting," pp. 25-26.

48. For a discussion of the relation of the image of St. Joseph to that of patriarchs of indigenous Andean mythology, see Christopher Wilson, "Beyond Strong Men and Frontiers: Conquests of the Spanish Mystics," in *Temples of Gold, Crowns of Silver,* pp. 124-25.

49. Barbara von Barghahn analyzes the style of painting which arose in Cuzco after the Indian artists broke away from the Spanish guilds, relating it to traditional Inca styles of design, in "A Silver Age of Colonial Latin America: The Viceregal Andes and the Persistence of Tradition," in *The 1992 Washington Antiques Show, Quincentennial Commemorative Catalogue* (Washington, D.C., 1992), pp. 101-07.

50. Mesa and Gisbert, *Historia,* p. 141.

51. For a discussion of the important influence of Flemish engravings, including a chart matching *cuzqueña* paintings with their print sources, see Mesa and Gisbert, *Historia,* pp. 101-10.

52. Peers, *Handbook,* p. 116.

53. Peers, *Handbook,* p. 118.

54. Baldomero Jiménez Duque, *Ana de San Bartolomé* (Madrid: Editorial de Espiritualidad, 1979), pp. 19-20.

55. John B. Knipping, *Iconography of the Counter Reformation in the Netherlands: Heaven on Earth,* 2 vols. (Nieuwkoop: B. de Graaf and Leiden: A.W. Sijthoff, 1974), 1:117, note 56.

56. Knipping, 1:117.

Just Man, Husband of Mary, and Guardian of Christ: St. Joseph's Life and Virtues in the Spirituality of St. Francis de Sales

Joseph F. Chorpenning, O.S.F.S.

The spirituality of St. Francis de Sales is embodied in two primary historical forms. One is in Francis' person and writings, the most important and well-known being the *Introduction to the Devout Life* (1609) and the *Treatise on the Love of God* (1616) (Pl. 1). The other is found in the person of St. Jane Frances de Chantal and the religious community of the Visitation of Holy Mary that was co-founded by Francis and Jane (Pl. 2).[1] This essay focuses on Francis' contribution to the development of devotion to St. Joseph via his writings and the Visitation.

PLATE 1.

St. Francis de Sales Composing the "Treatise on the Love of God." Engraving from *La vie du venerable serviteur de Dieu François de Sales...* (Paris: Nicolas Belley, 1707).

In 1923, in the encyclical *Rerum Omnium* that commemorated the third centenary of Francis' death, Pope Pius XI proclaimed him as the patron of journalists and Catholic writers. This proclamation could not have been more apropos, for not only after his death but during his lifetime Francis was a best-selling author. The success of the *Introduction* was so great and immediate that during Francis' lifetime it was translated into several of the principal European languages: Latin (1612), English (1613), Spanish (1618), and Italian (1621, although there may have been another as early as 1610).[2] By 1656 this work had been translated into seventeen languages. Although neither as popular nor as widely translated as the *Introduction*, the *Treatise* was translated into the major European languages after Francis' death: English (1630), Italian (1642), Latin (1643), Spanish (1661), German (1661), and Polish (1751).[3]

Francis' writings enjoyed great popularity in the Hispanic world. For example, the translator and editor of the standard modern Spanish translation of Francis' works reports that the Biblioteca Nacional in Madrid contains, among others, copies of the following Spanish translations: five seventeenth-century editions, twelve eighteenth-century editions, and six nineteenth-century editions of the *Introduction*; three seventeenth-century editions and three eighteenth-century editions of Francis' *Letters*; one seventeenth-century edition and two eighteenth-century editions of the *Spiritual Conferences* that Francis gave to the Sisters of the Visitation (Pl. 3); and two eighteenth-century editions of selected sermons.[4] Another indication of Francis' popularity in the Spanish-speaking world is the publication in the late seventeenth-century by the Madrid printer Antonio Román of two works about Francis: first, in 1688, the Spanish translation by Francisco Cubillas and Pedro Godoy of Adrien Gambart's 1664 book of fifty-two emblems depicting symbolically Francis' life (Pl. 4), and, second, in 1695, Miguel de la Portilla's Spanish biography of Francis (Pl. 5).[5] Finally, it is noteworthy that, in his recent masterful study of the iconography of Spanish American Baroque art, the Spanish art historian Santiago Sebastián López calls attention to the role Francis' writings played in the diffusion of devotion to St. Joseph.[6]

PLATE 2.

St. Francis de Sales Giving the Rule of the Visitation of Holy Mary to St. Jane Frances de Chantal. Engraving from *La vie du venerable serviteur de Dieu François de Sales...* (Paris: Nicolas Belley, 1707).

St. Teresa of Ávila's writings give abundant testimony to the patronage and intercessory power of St. Joseph in her life and religious experience.[7] Having read Teresa's works in French translation, Francis would have certainly been aware of the Mother of Carmel's intense devotion to St. Joseph.[8] In fact, it is reported that Francis often said that he had special devotion to Teresa because of all she did to foster and to disseminate devotion to St. Joseph through her reform of Carmel.[9] There is much evidence that Francis was personally devoted

PLATE 3.
Title-page of the 1740 Spanish edition of the *Spiritual Conferences*.

to St. Joseph. For example, the only image that he carried in his breviary was a picture of St. Joseph; he fasted on the vigil of St. Joseph's feast day and always preached on his feast (March 19); at Mass he often put in St. Joseph's name; he placed a dedicatory prayer to St. Joseph at the beginning of the *Treatise;* he dedicated the first church that he built in Annecy to St. Joseph; he composed a litany of St. Joseph for the Visitandines as well as placed them under this saint's patronage.[10] However, the primary form that Francis' writings on St. Joseph take is not personal testimony, but "solid theological analysis in a devotional format."[11] Frequently Francis' method will be akin to that of medieval and early modern meditative practices, the *locus classicus* of which are the "composition of place" and the "application of the senses" in St. Ignatius Loyola's *Spiritual Exercises*.[12] By means of these practices, the exercitant recreates in the imagination sacred events and participates in them. The meditator is to visualize the material place where the mystery to be considered occurred, e.g., its length, breadth, size, height, arrangement. Next, one is to make oneself part of the scene by observing those present, by contemplating what occurs, by imagining what is heard, smelled, felt. In his reflection on the events of St. Joseph's life that are found in Scripture and in pious tradition, Francis seeks to recreate them for his audience by suggesting Joseph's thoughts, feelings, and conversation in order to make these events tangible and to draw out their deepest spiritual meaning and relevance for his readers/listeners.

ST. JOSEPH AS MODEL OF THE DEVOUT LIFE IN THE LAY STATE

Francis' spirituality is grounded in the fundamental conviction that God extends to all—layperson or cleric, man or woman, celibate or married—an invitation to divine union which can be realized not only in the desert or monastery but anywhere. For Francis, union with God, for which the human person is created, does not require withdrawal or flight from the world or human society. Anticipating the Second Vatican Council's universal call to holiness by four centuries, Francis affirms that the vast majority of Christians are called to this union in the busyness of the world and amidst the obligations of marriage and family life. This union is effected by devotion: prompt, active, and faithful obedience to God's commandments, counsels, and inspirations.

PLATE 4.
Title-page of the 1688 Spanish edition of Adrien Gambart's book of fifty-two emblems depicting symbolically the life of St. Francis de Sales.

The manifesto of this fundamental conviction of Salesian spirituality is the *Introduction*. In Part I, chapter 3, Francis unequivocally states the thesis of this work: "It is an error, or rather a heresy, to wish to banish the devout life from the regiment of soldiers, the mechanic's shop, the court of princes, or the home of married people" (p. 44). To support his thesis, Francis lists two dozen people from the Bible and Christian history who achieved perfection in the lay state. St. Joseph heads the list of examples from the Christian era. Undoubtedly it is on account of his many virtues that St. Joseph epitomizes the devout life in the lay state. In the *Introduction*, however, Francis discusses only one of Joseph's virtues. In Part III, chapter 28, the topic of which is rash judgment, the Bishop of Geneva considers St. Joseph's comportment toward his espoused wife when he discovers her to be pregnant. Historically Joseph's conduct on this occasion has had three principal interpretations: first, that Joseph actually suspected Mary of adultery (St. Augustine); second, that he surmised that Mary was the mother of the Messiah, and he wished to withdraw in humility (St. Bernard); and, third, that he was subjected to agonizing perplexity (Francisco Suárez).[13] Although elsewhere Francis follows the opinions of Bernard and Suárez, here he offers another interpretation.

> If an action has many different aspects, we must always think of which is the best. Our Lady was with child and St. Joseph clearly saw this fact. On the other hand, he saw that she was all holy, all pure, all angelic, and he could never believe that

she had conceived in an unlawful manner. Hence he resolved to leave her and leave judgment on her case to God. Although there was strong argument leading him to form an ill opinion of the Virgin, he would never pass judgment on her. Why? Because, says the Spirit of God, "he was a just man." When a just man can no longer explain either the fact or the intention of someone whom he otherwise knows to be virtuous, he still will not pass judgment on him but puts it out of his mind and leaves the judgment to God (p. 199).[14]

VIVA JESUS.
VIDA
VIRTUDES, Y MILAGROS
DEL GLORIOSO SEÑOR
S. FRANCISCO DE SALES.
NATURAL DEL DUCADO
DE SABOYA,
OBISPO, Y PRINCIPE DE GINEBRA.
Patriarca de la Orden Sagrada de las Religiosas de la Visitacion: Tercero de los Minimos de S. Francisco de Paula: de la Congregacion del Oratorio en Tonon.
Con dos Indices de Capitulos y de Cosas Notables.
QUE DEDICA
AL EMIN.mo Y REV.mo SEÑOR DON LUIS MANUEL Portocarrero, Cardenal de la Santa Iglesia de Roma, del Titulo de Santa Sabina, Protector de España, Arçobispo de Toledo, Primado de las Españas, Canciller Mayor de Castilla, del Consejo de Estado de su Magestad, &c.
SU AUTOR
EL PADRE DOCTOR DON MIGUEL DE LA PORTILLA,
CON PRIVILEGIO.
En Madrid: En la Imprenta de ANTONIO ROMAN. Año de 1695.

PLATE 5.
Title-page of Miguel de la Portilla's Spanish biography of St. Francis de Sales (1695).

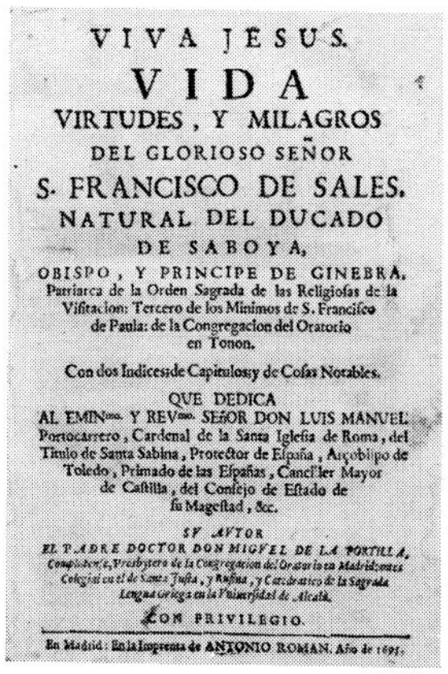

For discussion of the rest of St. Joseph's virtues, we must turn to the *Spiritual Conferences.*

Francis' 1622 Sermon on St. Joseph

There are passing references to St. Joseph throughout the corpus of Francis' writings. In the four volumes of his sermons in the Annecy edition of his complete works, there are two outlines for sermons Francis preached on the feast of St. Joseph (1612, 1614) and the text of the sermon for St. Joseph's feast, 1621, which Francis delivered in the church of the Jesuit novitiate in Lyons.[15] Francis' most extensive and complete treatment of St. Joseph is Conference 19 in the *Spiritual Conferences.* This conference was a sermon preached by Francis on the feast of St. Joseph to the sisters of the Visitation in Annecy in 1622, the last year of his life. It is entitled "On the Virtues of St. Joseph" and develops fully as well as incorporates material from the sermon Francis preached in Lyons the previous year (Pl. 6). Francis also speaks at length about St. Joseph in Conference 3, "On Constancy," another sermon preached to the Visitandines for the octave of the feast of the Holy Innocents.

Although Conference 19 is almost always referred to, and selected passages are often quoted, in scholarship on Francis' contribution to the development of St. Joseph's cult, it has not been systematically studied in its entirety.[16] The greater part of the rest of this essay will offer an exposition and analysis of this sermon, clearly Francis' definitive statement on St. Joseph. This presentation will be supplemented by Francis' discussion of St. Joseph in other writings, specifically Conference 3 and the *Treatise.*

De las virtudes de San Joseph. 215
VIVA JESUS.
ENTRETENIMIENTO XIX.
Sobre las virtudes de San Joseph.

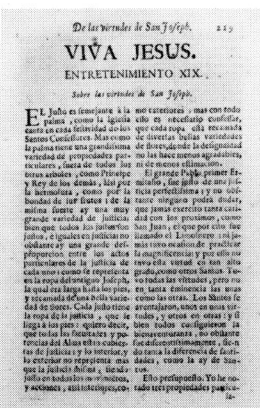

PLATE 6.
First page of St. Francis de Sales' sermon "On the Virtues of St. Joseph" in the 1740 Spanish edition of the *Spiritual Conferences.*

St. Joseph's Unique Ministry in the Holy Family

At the outset of Conference 19, Francis observes that each confessor-saint is, as the Church proclaims in the introit for the common of confessors, a just man who flourishes like the palm tree (cf. Psalm 92.13). These just men are garbed in a robe like that "of the Patriarch Joseph, which descended to his feet, and was embroidered with a rich variety of flowers" (p. 364). According to Francis, the flowers which adorn the robes of these confessors are the different virtues of each saint. St. Joseph is preeminent not only among confessors but all the other saints. He is "not only a Patriarch, but the chief and leader of Patriarchs; he is not simply a Confessor, but more than a Confessor, for in him are enshrined the worth of Bishops, the generosity of Martyrs, and of all the other saints" (p. 365). Hence St. Joseph wears a robe embroidered with the flowers of his virtues, making him comparable to the Old Testament Patriarch Joseph.[17] The portrait of St. Joseph that Francis paints in words here may have contributed to the practice in Spanish American Colonial art of decorating St. Joseph's garment with gold patterning, a form of decoration which recovered "the aesthetic of the first Hispano-Flemish paintings that arrived in America with their gilded overlays."[18] In fact, St. Joseph's robe was decorated with more elaborate patterning than that of any other saint (see, e.g., Wilson, Pl. 10, von Barghahn, Pl. 16, and Catalogue 11, 15).

To expound on St. Joseph's particular virtues, Francis returns to the image of the palm, "the king of trees" (p. 365). Joseph can be compared to the palm tree on three counts: first, his chastity; second, his humility; and, third, his combination of courage, constancy, and strength. The palm tree was one of the most popular and ubiquitous images in Renaissance art and literature. The sources for the rich complex of meanings that were associated with the palm tree were the authors of classical antiquity, the Bible, and medieval exegesis and preaching.[19] Francis freely draws upon this complex in his comparison of St. Joseph and the palm.

One of the salient characteristics of the palm is that while it has gender, it produces its fruit virginally. According to Aristotle and Pliny, only the female palm bears dates as its fruit; however, for it to do so it must be planted not only near, but in the sight of, the male palm. Although the male contributes none of its substance to the female's production, it cannot be said that it does not share in the female's fruit because without the male the female would remain barren and unfruitful. Francis regards St. Joseph as comparable to the palm because

> although he contributed nothing of his own [to Mary's "holy and glorious fruit"], he had a great part in this most holy fruit of his sacred Spouse. She belonged to him, and was planted close to him, like a glorious palm by the side of its beloved palm-tree, and, according to the decree of divine Providence, could not produce fruit, and must not do so except under his shadow and in his sight; I mean, under the shadow of the holy marriage which they had contracted together. . . . Oh! divine union between Our Lady and the glorious St. Joseph! By means of this union that Good of eternal goods, Our Lord Himself, belonged to St. Joseph as well as to Our Lady (p. 367).

Two points in this passage merit comment.

First, Francis uses the comparison of the palm to cast into relief St. Joseph's chastity. As the Bishop of Geneva explains, St. Joseph was

> the being who approached most nearly to [the] perfection [of our Lady]. . . . If the Blessed Virgin was not only a virgin all-pure and all-spotless, but even virginity itself . . ., how great and super-eminent in this virtue must not he have been who was appointed by the Eternal Father to be the guardian, or, to speak more truly, the companion of her virginity . . .? (pp. 368-69).

Fundamental to St. Joseph's preeminence is his true, virginal marriage to the Mother of God. "Jesus is the fruit of this marriage not because He was generated by means of it, but because He was received and reared within it according to God's reason for bringing it into existence."[20]

Second, Francis sees St. Joseph as an intimate and privileged participant in the life of Jesus and of Mary. Francis' contemporary, the Jesuit theologian Francisco Suárez (1548-1617), analyzed St. Joseph's place in the Holy Family by saying that the saint had a true though subordinate role in the order of the hypostatic union because of his unique ministry to Jesus and Mary.[21] Francis does not use this technical theological language to speak of Joseph's role in the Holy Family. Rather, he has recourse to the language of images and of affectivity. Wendy M. Wright has observed of Francis' literary style:

> His prose is notable for its gracious use of metaphor, the unexpected turn of phrase and image. This aesthetic is not some mere ornament upon his thought but the vessel which gives form to content and upon which the particular nature of his thought depends for transmission.[22]

Farther on in this conference, Francis deftly weaves the images of the dove, *hortus conclusus* (enclosed garden), date, and palm tree into an allegory to represent how Mary's parenthood was shared with Joseph since she belonged to him as his wife and since the procreation of the Child Jesus in her, even though virginal, belonged to Joseph's marriage.

> If a dove . . . carried in her beak a date which she let fall into a garden, would you not say that the palm-tree which sprang up from the date belonged to the owner of the garden? Well, if that is so, who can doubt that the Holy Ghost, like a holy Dove, having let fall this divine date into the enclosed and shut-up garden of the Blessed Virgin . . . which belonged to St. Joseph as the bride to her husband— who can doubt, I repeat, that this divine palm-tree, which bears fruits of immortal nourishment, belongs most truly to St. Joseph . . . ? (pp. 377-78).

A modern author has written of St. Joseph's role in the Holy Family:

> Joseph thus became the only human being who ever received the filial love of Jesus Christ and the all-chaste conjugal love of the Blessed Virgin. His privileged position placed him even above the Apostles and John the Baptist, for he lived in a different and superior order—his was the circle of intimacy with Jesus and Mary which no one else ever entered, the "hypostatic order."[23]

In the dedicatory prayer to St. Joseph in the *Treatise,* Francis describes the affectionate relationship between Jesus and Joseph in a manner that this text could serve as a commentary on the numerous portraits of Joseph and the Christ Child in European and Spanish American Colonial art.

> Great St. Joseph, most beloved spouse of the Mother of the Beloved, ah, how many times have you borne in your arms the love of heaven and earth! All the while, inflamed by the sweet embrace and kiss of that divine child, your soul was dissolved in joy. All the while—O God, how sweet it was!—he spoke tenderly into your ears and told you that you were his great friend and his beloved father (1: 34).

St. Joseph's Dignity and Humility

A second characteristic that St. Joseph and the palm share in common is humility. Francis writes:

> For although the palm is the prince of trees, it is nevertheless the humblest, and the proof of this is that it hides its flowers in the springtime, when all other trees are displaying theirs, and does not put them forth till the summer heat is at its height. The palm keeps its blossoms shut up in little bags in the form of a sheath . . . (p. 371).

The difference between the palm and other trees is like that between the worldly and earthly-minded and the just, of whom Joseph is the preeminent example. When the former have a good thought or are stirred by virtue, they "become restlessly eager to display it and publish it abroad to all whom they may meet" (p. 371). Trees that are hasty in putting forth their blossoms in springtime are in danger of being surprised by a frost, and hence having their blossoms perish and bearing no fruit. Likewise, the proud and amibitious of the world who "put forth all their blossoms in the springtime of this mortal life, always run the risk of being struck by a frost which destroys the fruit of their actions" (p. 372). By contrast, the just "keep their blossoms—that is, their virtues—hidden under the veil of humility until death, when Our Lord suffers them to burst forth and be seen by all, being speedily followed by their fruits" (p. 372). St. Joseph epitomizes this humility.

St. Joseph was the guardian of Christ, his reputed father, and the husband of our Lady. Francis regards St. Joseph as being "more valiant than David and wiser than Solomon" (p. 373). The Bishop of Geneva observes of the divine election of St. Joseph:

> If earthly princes consider it a matter of so much importance to select carefully a tutor fit for their children, think you that the Eternal God would not, in His almighty power and wisdom, choose from out of the whole of His creation the most perfect man living to be the guardian of His divine and most glorious Son, the Prince of heaven and earth? (p. 373).

Following Jean Gerson, the great medieval theologian, Chancellor of the Sorbonne, and promoter of St. Joseph's cult whom the Bishop of Geneva greatly admired,[24] Francis avers that Jesus, Mary, and Joseph formed "a trinity on earth representing in some sort the most holy Trinity" (p. 374). The theme of the Holy Family as the earthly trinity was extemely popular in European and Spanish American Colonial painting (see Catalogue 12).

However great though Joseph's dignity was, he lived his earthly life in poverty, abjection, and humility. Francis remarks:

> One instance alone is sufficient to prove this; he went into his own country and to his own town of Bethlehem, and, as far as we know, he alone was refused admittance into any of the inns, so that he was constrained to retire, and to conduct his most chaste Spouse into a stable among oxen and asses (p. 374).

St. Joseph's humility is also evident in his conduct when he learned of Mary's pregnancy. In this instance Francis not only agrees with, but quotes, Bernard's interpretation: Joseph surmised that Mary was the mother of the Messiah, and he wished to withdraw in humility.

> His humility also, as St. Bernard explains, was the cause of his wishing to quit Our Lady when he saw that she was with child; for St. Bernard says that he spoke thus to himself: "Ah! what is this? I know that she is a virgin, for we have together made a vow to keep our virginity and purity intact—a vow which nothing would induce her to break; yet I see that she is with child. How can it be that maternity is found in virginity, and that virginity does not hinder maternity? O my God! must not this be that glorious Virgin of whom the Prophets declare that she shall conceive and be the Mother of the Messiah? Oh, if this is so, God forbid that I should remain with her—I, who am so unworthy of such an honour! Better far that I should quit her secretly on account of my unworthiness, and that I should dwell no longer in her company" (pp. 374-75).

Finally, Francis imagines that "the Angels, wondering and adoring, came thronging in countless multitudes" (p. 373) to Joseph's poor workshop to admire his humility. St. Joseph's humility was "a box of alabaster" (p. 376) that protected and preserved the precious ointment of his other virtues, especially chastity.

St. Joseph's Courage, Constancy, and Perseverance

The third attribute of the palm that is found in St. Joseph is its union of courage, constancy, and strength. This property of the palm was frequently depicted in seventeenth-century emblem books. The Bishop of Geneva's explanation of this attribute serves as an apt commentary on emblem forty-three in Gambart's book that depicts how although the weight of the world falls upon it, the palm neither yields nor breaks (Pl. 7).

> The palm has a strength, courage, and even constancy far beyond all other trees, therefore it takes the highest rank among them. The palm shows its strength in this, that the more it is laden, the more it shoots up and the higher it grows; which is quite unlike all other trees, and indeed all other things, for the more heavily they are laden, the more they bow down to the earth. The palm, however, shows its strength and constancy, never bending down, whatever load is placed upon it. It is its instinct to shoot upwards, and nothing can prevent it from doing so. It shows its valour in its sword-shaped foliage, and seems, therefore, to have as many weapons of defence as it has leaves (p. 378).

St. Joseph also possessed these related yet distinct virtues: constancy, perseverance, strength, and valor.

St. Joseph displayed constancy when he discovered that Mary was pregnant. Here Francis follows another of the principal interpretations of St. Joseph's conduct on this occasion: he was subjected to agonizing perplexity. Francis observes: although St. Joseph's "mind was tossed with distress, perplexity, and trouble . . . he never complained, he was never harsh or ungracious towards his holy Spouse, but remained just as gentle and respectful in his demeanour as he had ever been" (p. 379).

In Conference 3, "On Constancy," Francis offers St. Joseph's entire life as a model of constancy in the midst of the vicissitudes of human life. Joseph's life, as every human life, was filled with inconstancy, that is, a mixture of joys and sorrows, of consolation and grief. For example, the affliction and distress of Joseph's discovery of Mary's pregnancy was followed by the consolation of the Lord's birth that was followed by the grief of the flight into Egypt. St. Joseph's anchor and center of gravity amidst this inconstancy was his unfailing trust in, and obedience to, the will of God. This trust and obedience is manifested in Joseph's immediate reponse to the angelic commands to take Mary as his wife and to flee into Egypt.

St. Joseph's valor and strength is revealed by his humility, a topic which Francis has just discussed at length. Now, however, Francis develops his point from a different perspective.

Humility is odious to the devil, who was expelled from heaven and cast into hell because of his lack of humility. St. Joseph must have resisted fierce assaults upon his humility by the devil, for "there is no artifice or invention he will not use to make men fall away from [humility] because it is a virtue which renders them infinitely pleasing to God" (p. 380).

The virtue of St. Joseph to which Francis devotes the most attention in this section is perservance, which is defined as follows:

> Perseverance . . . has chiefly to do with a certain weariness of mind which comes upon us when we have suffered a long time, and this weariness is as powerful an enemy as we can meet with. Now, perseverance enables a man so to disregard this enemy that he gains the victory over it by continual calmness and submission to the will of God (p. 379).

By his perseverance, St. Joseph overcame "weariness and dejection under the continued assaults of humbling, painful circumstances—ill fortune, as we say—and the thousand accidents and misadventures of daily life" (p. 380). Joseph's perseverance is especially evident in his conduct during the episode of the flight into Egypt.

PLATE 7. Emblem 43 in the Spanish translation of Gambart (1688).

St. Joseph obeyed the angel's command to set forth immediately with Mary and the Christ Child for Egypt without hesitation or question. Certainly he must have been oppressed by "dejection and distress of mind . . . since the Angel had not told him how long a time he must remain in Egypt, and he could not settle down in any fixed abode, not knowing when he might be commanded to return" (pp. 380-81). Moreover, Egypt "was . . . a land not only strange but hostile to the Israelites, inasmuch as the Egyptians resented the fact of their having escaped from their tyranny, and also of their having been the cause of many of their nation being drowned in the depths of the Red Sea, when in pursuit of them" (p. 381). St. Joseph was "perfectly united to the divine will, and . . . always conformed to it, in all sorts of events, whether prosperous or adverse" (p. 382). For Francis, St. Joseph's prompt and perfect obedience to the divine will not only imitates but emulates Abraham's obedience (p. 381; cf. pp. 47, 52).

The virtue of perseverance is also seen in St. Joseph's practice of the virtue of poverty.

> Every one looked upon this Saint as a poor carpenter. Though he toiled with the most affectionate zeal for the support of his little family, yet he could not earn enough to prevent their wanting many necessary things. . . . Then, as the years went on, and his poverty and abjection continued, he still submitted always most humbly to the will of God. He never allowed himself to be conquered or subdued by dejection of mind, which yet, no doubt, constantly attacked him (pp. 382-83).

Here Francis provides a firm basis for St. Joseph's invocation as patron of workers and of parents who struggle to provide the basic necessities of life for their families.

St. Joseph's Death, Assumption, and Heavenly Intercession

Up to this point Francis' theological reflection on St. Joseph is based on the events of his life recorded in Scripture: his discovery of Mary's pregnancy, the Nativity of our Lord, the flight into Egypt. Francis concludes his sermon by considering St. Joseph's heavenly intercession and assumption into heaven. However, before turning to these topics, it is appropriate to consider Francis' discussion of St. Joseph's death in the *Treatise*.

Since the seventeenth century St. Joseph has been invoked as patron of the dying.[25] Francis' reflection on St. Joseph's death in the *Treatise*, Book 7, chapter 13, gives a solid theological foundation for this aspect of his cult as well as for the frequent depiction of this event in European and Spanish American Colonial art (Pl. 8). Francis regards it as certain that Joseph died before Jesus' passion and death because otherwise Jesus would not have placed his Mother in the care of the Beloved Disciple (John 19.26-27). The Bishop of Geneva envisions Joseph dying, assisted by, and in the arms of, Jesus.

> Ah, how much sweetness, charity, and mercy did this good foster father show towards the Savior when he was born into the world as a little child! Who then can have any doubt that when he left this world that divine Son rendered the same services to him, multiplied a hundred times, and that he filled him with heavenly joy? . . . While our Savior was still a little child, the great St. Joseph, his foster father, and the most glorious Virgin, his Mother, had carried him many times, especially on the journey they made from Judea into Egypt, and then from Egypt back to Judea. Ah, who can doubt that when this holy father came to the end of his years, he in turn was carried by his divine foster Child on his journey from this world into the next, into Abraham's bosom, from there to be translated into the Son's own bosom, into glory, on the day of his Ascension? (2: 48-49).

According to Francis, the cause of Joseph's death, like that of the Virgin Mary, St. Francis of Assisi, St. Teresa of Ávila, and other great servants of God, was love.

> A saint who had loved so much in this life could not die except from love. His soul could not sufficiently love his own dear Jesus amid all the distractions of this life, and he had already performed the services required of him during the childhood of Jesus. What remained, then, but for him to say to the eternal Father, "O Father, I have accomplished the work which you have given me to do," and then to the Son, "O my Child, as your heavenly Father placed your tender body in my hands on the day you came into the world, so do I place my spirit in your hands on this day of my departure from this world" (2:49).

One of the great disputed questions in the history of devotion to St. Joseph is that of the saint's resurrection and assumption into heaven. Gerson, St. Bernardine of Siena, and Suárez had presented positive arguments for Joseph's assumption. However, "[no] one has ever proposed the doctrine more vigorously than Francis de Sales."[26] Francis puts forth this opinion at the end of Conference 19 as theologically probable and on the grounds of fitness.

> What more remains to be said, except that we can never for a moment doubt that this glorious Saint has great influence in heaven with Him Who raised him there in body and in soul—a fact which is the more probable because we have no relic of that body left to us here below! Indeed, it seems to me that no one can doubt this as a truth, for how could He Who had been so obedient to St. Joseph, all through His life, refuse him this grace? Doubtless when Our Lord descended into Limbo He was accosted by St. Joseph in words like these: "O my Lord, remember, if it please Thee, that when Thou didst come down from heaven to earth, I received Thee into my house and my family and that at the moment of Thy birth I received Thee into mine arms. Now that Thou art returning to heaven, take me there with Thee; I received Thee into my family, receive me now into Thine. I have carried Thee in my arms, take me into Thine; and as I carefully nourished and protected Thee in Thy mortal life, take care of me and lead me into life immortal." And if it is true, as we are bound to believe, that in virtue of the Blessed Sacrament which we receive, our bodies will come to life again in the day of judgment, how could we doubt that Our Lord raised up to heaven, in body and soul, the glorious St. Joseph? For he had the honour and the grace of carrying Him so often in his blessed arms, those arms in which Our Lord took so much pleasure. Oh, how many and what tender kisses His sacred lips bestowed on him, to reward him for his toil and labours! (pp. 383-84).

In the *Introduction* Francis tells his reader that, among others, St. Joseph, who lived devotion in the world and is now part of the heavenly court, invites and encourages us in our election of the devout life (pp. 70, 273). Francis concludes the final sermon he would preach on St. Joseph by emphasizing the power of his heavenly intercession. Gerson held that St. Joseph's intercessory power in heaven was unbounded: "he rather commands than supplicates."[27] Francis concurs: "Oh, how happy shall we be if we can merit a share in [St. Joseph's] holy intercession! for nothing will be refused to him either by Our Lady or by her glorious Son" (p. 384). Through the intercession of Joseph, "growth in all virtues, but especially in those which . . . he possesses in a higher degree than any other man," specifically "great purity of body and mind, humility, constancy, courage, and perseverance" (p. 384) can be obtained. The virtues epitomized by St. Joseph "make us victorious in this life over our enemies, and through them we shall merit the grace to enjoy in eternal life the rewards prepared for those who shall imitate the example given by St. Joseph whilst in this life—a reward which will be nothing less than eternal happiness, in which we shall enjoy the unclouded vision of the Father, the Son, and the Holy Ghost" (pp. 384-85).

DEVOTION TO ST. JOSEPH IN THE VISITATION

For Francis, the response to the invitation to divine union in whatever state of life is enfleshed by the practice of what he calls in the third part of the *Introduction* "those little virtues." Francis exhorts:

> Let us try sincerely, humbly, and devoutly to acquire those little virtues whose conquest our Savior has set forth as the end of our care and labor. Such are patience, meekness, self-mortification, humility, obedience, poverty, chastity, tenderness toward our neighbors, bearing with their imperfections, diligence, and holy fervor (p. 127).

PLATE 8.

Javier Cortés (Ecuador), *The Death of St. Joseph*, 1778. Tercera Orden Franciscana Seglar, Lima (Jorge Bernales Ballesteros).

The Bishop of Geneva sought to inculcate these virtues both in his directees in the world and in the sisters of the Visitation. Conference 19 makes it clear that St. Joseph's life is the example *par excellence* of the practice of the "little virtues."

It is surely no coincidence that Francis preached on St. Joseph's virtues to the Visitandines. Francis holds St. Joseph up to his spiritual daughters as the model for the perfect religious. Francis also chose St. Joseph as special patron of the Order of the Visitation and the particular patron of each monastery. It has been observed of Francis' transmission of his devotion to St. Joseph to the Visitation: "He desired that this devotion, which he had himself so strongly imbibed, might also serve his first daughters of the Visitation as a spiritual food, well caculated to strengthen and improve them in the interior life."[28] Indeed, Francis wished that, after the Virgin Mary, St. Joseph occupy the first place in the affections and confidence of the Visitandines. Francis also desired that St. Joseph have a primary place in the devotional life of the Visitation. For example, as we know from Francis' letter of March 19, 1614, to Jane de Chantal, he composed a litany of St. Joseph to be sung by the nuns. Unfortunately there is no extant copy of this litany.[29]

> My dearest daughter, here is the Litany of the glorious father of our life and of our love. I intended to send you it written with my own hand, but, as you know, I am not myself. Still I have taken the time to revise it, to correct and to put in the accents, that our daughter de Chastel may more easily sing it without making mistakes.
>
> But you, my daughter, who will not be able to sing the praises of this Saint of our heart, you will ruminate them, like the spouse, between your teeth; that is, while your mouth is closed your heart will be open to the meditation of the greatnesses of this spouse of the Queen of all the world, named father of Jesus, and his first adorer, after his divine Spouse.[30]

In accord with Francis' own wishes, to the present century various devotions to St. Joseph are practiced by the Visitation, including the sorrows and joys of St. Joseph, the beads of St. Joseph, a daily offering to St. Joseph, an offering to St. Joseph for the month of March, and the litany of St. Joseph.[31] Thus Francis' contribution to the development of devotion to St. Joseph may be said to have been disseminated through two primary historical forms: his writings, the publication and great popularity of which antedated the foundation of Visitation monasteries in Spain and in the New World;[32] and the Visitation, which has kept alive Francis' fervent personal devotion to, and affection for, St. Joseph.

CONCLUSION

For Francis, the just man St. Joseph achieved sanctity by unfailing fidelity to the duties of his state of life as husband of our Lady and guardian of Christ. In the midst of constant adversity, St. Joseph was a man of faith, obedience to God's will, charity, humility, fortitude, constancy, and perseverance. Francis regards St. Joseph as a model for Christians both in the world and in religious life. Moreover, Francis' solid theological analysis of Joseph's life and virtues provides a firm foundation for his subsequent declaration in papal documents and popular acclaim as patron of the Universal Church, families and family life, parents, religious, workers, travelers, the poor, and the dying. Finally, Francis' writings on St. Joseph offer eloquent commentary to accompany the numerous depictions of St. Joseph and the Christ Child and of the Holy Family in European and Spanish American Colonial art.

Notes

1. Wendy M. Wright and Joseph F. Power, O.S.F.S., "Introduction" to Francis de Sales and Jane de Chantal, *Letters of Spiritual Direction,* translated by Péronne Marie Thibert, V.H.M., The Classics of Western Spirituality (New York: Paulist Press, 1988), pp. 9-86, at p. 12. Wright's and Power's introduction provides an excellent overview of the themes of Salesian spirituality. For a briefer treatment of the same, see Joseph F. Chorpenning, O.S.F.S., "Salesian Spirituality," in *The New Dictionary of Catholic Spirituality,* ed. Michael Downey (Collegeville: The Liturgical Press, 1992).

2. See John K. Ryan's introduction to his translation of St. Francis de Sales, *Introduction to the Devout Life* (Garden City: Image Books, 1972), p. 17. All subsequent references to the *Introduction* are to this translation.

3. See John K. Ryan's introduction to his translation of St. Francis de Sales, *Treatise on the Love of God,* 2 vols. (1963; Rockford, Illinois: Tan Books, 1974-75), 1:27. All subsequent references to the *Treatise* are to this translation.

4. See *Obras selectas de San Francisco de Sales,* translated and edited by Francisco de la Hoz, S.D.B., 2 vols., Biblioteca de autores cristianos (Madrid: Editorial Católica, 1953-54), 1:xviii-xix.

5. The full titles of these works are: *Vida simbólica del glorioso S. Francisco de Sales, Obispo de Geneva, dividida en dos partes y escrita en cinquenta y dos emblemas* (Symbolic Life of the Glorious Saint Francis de Sales, Bishop of Geneva, Divided in Two Parts and Written in Fifty-Two Emblems) and *Vida, virtudes, y milagros del glorioso Señor S. Francisco de Sales, Natural del Ducado de Saboya, Obispo, y Príncipe de Ginebra, Patriarca de la Orden Sagrada de las Religiosas de la Visitación, Tercero de los Mínimos de S. Francisco de Paula, de la Congregación del Oratorio en Tonon* (Life, Virtues, and Miracles of the Glorious Lord St. Francis de Sales, Native of the Duchy of Savoy, Bishop, and Prince of Geneva, Patriarch of the Holy Order of the Religious of the Visitation, Religious of the Third Order of St. Francis of Paula, of the Congregation of the Oratory in Thonon). For further information on the former, see Pedro F. Campa, *Emblemata Hispanica: An Annotated Bibliography of Spanish Emblem Literature to the Year 1700* (Durham: Duke University Press, 1990), p. 98.

6. Santiago Sebastián López, *El barroco iberoamericano: Mensaje iconográfico* (Madrid: Ediciones Encuentro, 1990), p. 200.

7. The classic study of Teresa's devotion to St. Joseph is Fortunato de Jesús Sacramentado, O.C.D., "Santa Teresa de Jesús y su espíritu josefino," *Estudios Josefinos,* 7 (1953), 9-54. Also see Christopher C. Wilson, "St. Teresa of Ávila's Holy Patron: Teresian Sources for the Image of St. Joseph in Spanish American Colonial Art," in the present volume.

8. See Pierre Serouet, O.C.D., *De la vie dévote à la vie mystique: Sainte Thérèse d'Ávila, Saint François de Sales* (Paris: Desclée de Brouwer, 1958), pp. 17-134; Alphonse Vermeylen, *Sainte Thérèse en France au XVIIe siècle* (1600-1660) (Louvain: Publications Universitaires, 1958), pp. 92-111.

9. Serouet, p. 353.

10. *St. Francis de Sales: A Testimony by St. Chantal,* edited and translated by Elisabeth Stopp (Hyattsville, Maryland: Institute of Salesian Studies, 1967), pp. 74, 102; Louis Comte, *Saint Joseph, maître de vie spirituelle, d'aprés les oeuvres de Saint François de Sales* (Paris: P. Lethielleux, 1967), p. 30; *Treatise,* 1:34; Anthony-Joseph Patrignani, S.J., *A Manual of Practical Devotion to the Glorious Patriarch St. Joseph,* translated and revised by a Member of the Society of Jesus (1865; Rockford, Illinois: Tan Books, 1982), p. 78; and St. Francis de Sales, *Letters to Persons in Religion,* translated by Henry Benedict Mackey, O.S.B., 4th ed. (London: Burns & Oates, 1909), p. 419-20.

11. Francis L. Filas, S.J., *Joseph Most Just: Theological Questions about St. Joseph* (Milwaukee: Bruce Publishing Company, 1956), p. 112.

12. *The Spiritual Exercises of St. Ignatius,* translated by Louis J. Puhl, S.J. (Westminster, Maryland: Newman Press, 1951), pp. 25, 32-33.

13. Francis L. Filas, S.J., "Joseph, St., Devotion to," *New Catholic Encyclopedia,* 1967 edition.

14. Cf. *The Spiritual Conferences of St. Francis de Sales,* translated by F. Aidan Gasquet, O.S.B., and Henry Benedict Mackey, O.S.B. (1906; Westminster, Maryland: Newman Press, 1962), p. 72, note 8. All quotations from the *Conferences* are from this translation.

15. *Oeuvres de Saint François de Sales,* 26 vols. (Annecy: J. Niérat, 1892-1932), 8:86-88, 130-33, 397-402. Apropos of Francis' sermon of March 19, 1614, see André Doze's thoughtful reflection, "Les intuitions de S. François de Sales sur le mystère de saint Joseph," *Cahiers de Joséphologie,* 38 (1990), 211-23.

16. See, e.g., Filas, *Joseph Most Just,* pp. 53, 76, 111; Roland Gauthier, C.S.C., "Saint Joseph dans l'histoire de la spiritualité," *Dictionnaire de Spiritualité,* vol. 8 (Paris: Beauchesne, 1974), cols. 1308-16, especially cols. 1311-12; Henri-Paul Bergeron, C.S.C., "Saint Joseph dans la prédication française, de Saint François de Sales á Bossuet," *Cahiers de Joséphologie,* 29 (1981), 563-84, especially 564, 574, 580, 584; and Susan T. Stein, *The Tapestry of St. Joseph: Chronological History of St. Joseph and His Apostle, Blessed Brother André* (Philadelphia: Apostle Publishing, 1991), pp. 57-60. Comte's book (cited in note 10 above) is essentially an anthology of texts, arranged thematically and with minimum commentary, from Francis' works about St. Joseph. Although it includes selections from Conference 19, this sermon is not analyzed as a unit or in its totality.

17. One of St. Bernard's special contributions to the development of devotion to St. Joseph was his masterly comparison between the Patriarch Joseph and St. Joseph. After Bernard, this comparison became a commonplace. See Francis L. Filas, S.J., *The Man Nearest to Christ: Nature and Historic Development of the Devotion to St. Joseph* (Milwaukee: Bruce Publishing Company, 1944), p. 110. In his sermon outline for March 19, 1612, Francis compares the Patriarch Joseph and St. Joseph by applying the privileges of the former to the latter. See *Oeuvres,* 8:86-88.

18. Teresa Gisbert, "The Andean Gods throughout Christianity," in *Temples of Gold, Crowns of Silver: Reflections of Majesty in the Viceregal Americas,* edited by Barbara von Barghahn (Washington, D.C.: George Washington University, 1991), pp. 80-92, at p. 92.

19. For an excellent survey of this material, see J. M. Díaz de Bustamante, "*Onerata resurgit:* Notas a la tradición simbólica y emblemática de la palmera," *Helmantica,* 31, nos. 94-96 (1980), 27-88.

20. Filas, "Joseph, St., Devotion to." On the medieval debate whether or not a true marriage existed between Mary and Joseph, see Filas, *The Man Nearest to Christ,* pp. 111-14.

21. See Filas, *Joseph Most Just,* p. 29. "The word 'hypostatic' comes from the Greek language, and means 'personal.' Hence, because the divine and human nature were united in the one *person* of Jesus Christ, the order of the hypostatic union refers essentially to the human nature of Jesus together with all the gifts, privileges, and relationships that directly flow from it. Joseph and Mary also belong to the order of the hypostatic union, although not essentially but by reason of their ministries. Joseph's place lifts him above all other creatures because no one served Jesus and Mary more intimately than he" (Filas, *Joseph Most Just,* p. 29).

22. Wendy M. Wright, *Bond of Perfection: Jeanne de Chantal & François de Sales* (New York: Paulist Press, 1985), p. 66.

23. Filas, *The Man Nearest to Christ,* p. 88.

24. Serouet, p. 353, note 3. Gerson described the Holy Family as the "veneranda Trinitas" on earth. See John B. Knipping, *Iconography of the Counter Reformation in the Netherlands: Heaven on Earth,* 2 vols. (Leiden: A. W. Sijthoff, 1974), 1:114; and Christopher C. Wilson, "Beyond Strong Men and Frontiers: Conquests of the Spanish Mystics," in *Temples of Gold, Crowns of Silver,* pp. 116-27, especially p. 124.

25. David Hugh Farmer, *The Oxford Dictionary of Saints,* 2nd ed. (New York: Oxford University Press, 1987), p. 239; Keith P. Luria, "The Counter-Reformation and Popular Spirituality," in *Christian Spirituality: Post-Reformation and Modern,* edited by Louis Dupré and Don E. Saliers, World Spirituality: An Encyclopedic History of the Religious Quest, vol. 18 (New York: Crossroad, 1989), pp. 93-120, especially p. 114.

26. Filas, *Joseph Most Just,* pp. 75-76.

27. Quoted in Patrignani, p. 44.

28. Patrignani, p. 78. Also see Sebastián López , p. 200.

29. Roland Gauthier, C.S.C., "Les litanies de Saint Joseph au XVIIe siècle," *Cahiers de Joséphologie,* 35 (1987), 521-48, especially 526.

30. Letters to Persons in Religion, pp. 419-20.

31. *The Visitation Manual: A Collection of Prayers and Instructions Compiled according to the Spiritual Directory and Spirit of St. Francis de Sales, Founder of the Religious Order of the Visitation of Holy Mary* (New York: George Grady Press, 1955), pp. 414-23.

32. The first Visitation monastery in Spain was founded in Madrid from Annecy in 1749. Others followed: second monastery of Madrid (1798), Catalayud (1806), Orihuela (1826), Valladolid (1860), Barcelona (1874), Vitoria (1879), Valencia (1880), Pamplona (1881), Oviedo (1881), Burgos (1892), etc. The first foundation in the New World was Montevideo (1856), followed by Buenos Aires (1876), Santiago (1877), Lima (1891), Bogotà (1892), etc. See E. Bougaud, *St. Chantal and the Foundation of the Visitation,* translated from the 11th French edition by a Visitandine, 2 vols. (New York: Benziger Brothers, 1895), 2: 447-60.

From Prince to Sun King:
The Image of St. Joseph in Spain and the New World

Barbara von Barghahn

The Court of Madrid: Unveiling Josephine Metaphors in Portraits of the Hapsburg Prince

The art produced in Hapsburg Spain drew consistent analogies between images of the royal family and those of the Holy Family of Christ, Mary, and St. Joseph. In 1605 Juan Pantoja de la Cruz, court artist of Philip III (1598-1621), created *The Annunciation*, an allegorical painting containing a symbolical portrait of Queen Margarita of Austria (1584-1611).[1] The Spanish queen, who celebrated her birthday on December 25, sustained a lifelong devotion to the Virgin Mary (Pl. 1). Her fidelity culminated in the founding of the Royal Monastery of the Incarnation in Madrid. When the Madrilenian edifice was dedicated in 1611, it was referred to as "The Temple of the Annunciation." Following the wishes of Philip III and sanctioned by the Church, Pantoja de la Cruz portrayed Queen Margarita as *La Purísima* (Pl. 2). Her elevated image was complemented by the depiction of Princess Ana as the Archangel Gabriel bearing salutations from God. Presumably, *The Annunciation* portends the birth of Philip IV on April 8, 1605.[2] The genesis for this explicit conflation of secular and religious identities—the queen of an earthly realm with the *Regina Coeli*—may be found in late sixteenth-century art of the Hapsburg court.

PLATE 1. Juan Pantoja de la Cruz, *Queen Margarita of Austria*, 1606. Prado Museum, Madrid.

In 1575 Michele Parrasio, a disciple of Titian, was commissioned by Philip II to paint an *Allegory of the Birth of Prince Ferdinand* (Pl. 3).[3] Although the painting commemorated the birth of the Hapsburg heir on December 7, 1571, its iconography derived from ancient formulae concerning the birth of the sun god Apollo. Parrasio represented Latona with her newborn son, Phoebus-Apollo. Based upon the birth-narrative of the sun god recounted in the *Homeric Hymn to the Delian Apollo*, Phoebus's twin sister Diana-Lucina, assisted in his birth. Above Latona's canopy is a personification of Fame flanked by Diana-Lucina and Jupiter with an eagle. The arrow held by Latona is emblematic of the rays of the sun and the swift attainment of Fame. Heraclitus in his *Quaestiones Homericae* stated that the harmony of the spheres was based upon the arrows of Apollo.[4]

At the Spanish court, the myth of Latona recalled the judgment of Jupiter as recounted by Ovid in his *Metamorphoses* (6:317-381). In Greek mythology the mother of the infants Apollo and Diana was thirsty after much travelling. At the land of Lycia, they were prevented from drinking by some peasants, who were transformed into frogs for their lack of charity. Parrasio's allegory undeniably provides an association between Apollo and Prince Ferdinand, Latona and Queen Ana, and Jupiter and Philip II. A more complex analogy may be found in a Christian interpretation of the pagan theme.

PLATE 2. Juan Pantoja de la Cruz, *The Annunciation*, 1605. Kunsthistoriches Museum, Vienna.

Based upon Constantinian metaphors of the Messiah as the "dayspring on high," and the "rising sun," the newborn in Parrasio's work can be related to Christ, the "light shining in the darkness." Latona becomes the mythical counterpart to the Virgin Mary, and Philip II, the "Spanish Jupiter" in sixteenth-century pageantry, assumes a protective role similar to that of

PLATE 3.
Michele Parrasio, *Allegory of the Birth of Prince Ferdinand*, 1575. Prado Museum, Madrid.

St. Joseph. The birth of Apollo within the shelter of a tent, Latona's subsequent voyage, and the inhospitality of the Lycian peasants, evoke both the story of Joseph's vain search for an inn in Bethlehem and the flight into the arid land of Egypt (Pl. 4).[5]

The victory against the Turks at Lepanto on October 7, 1571, and the birth of Prince Ferdinand are celebrated in another allegorical work commissioned by Philip II, Titian's *Allegorical Portrait of Philip II after the Battle of Lepanto* (Pl. 5; called hereafter the *Allegory of Lepanto*). Based upon a drawing by the court portraitist Alonso Sánchez Coello that was sent to Venice, the painting was completed in 1575. After its arrival in Madrid, the work was displayed in the "Casa de Tesoro," a residence for foreign dignitaries belonging to the Alcázar Palace.[6] In 1625 the *Allegory of Lepanto* was transferred to the new audience room of the Alcázar, the "Hall of Mirrors." The court painter Vicencio Carducho added a bound Moor to the composition. Symbolic of the sublimation of discord, the figure suggested the emergence of a new "Golden Age," prophesied by Virgil in the *Fourth Ecologue of the Aeneid*.[7]

In the *Allegory of Lepanto*, Philip II corresponds to the description, in Erasmus's *Handbook of the Christian Knight* (1504), of the *miles christianus*, the source of which is Paul's letter to the Ephesians (6:10-16). Paul's letter concerns the conflict against the rulers of the "world of darkness," and the manner in which a Christian should be armed against the devil's deceits. Erwin Panofsky has observed that Philip II assumes the posture of a priest. Imitating the elevation of the consecrated host before an altar, the Spanish king dedicates his son to heaven.[8]

This liturgical imagery relates directly to the subject of Christ's Presentation in the Temple (Luke 2:22-39). St. Joseph brought the infant Jesus to the Temple of Jerusalem to be "consecrated to the Lord" (Pl. 6). Mosaic law required that the firstborn be sacrificed to the Lord, the child being redeemed by a token monetary payment. The rite commemorated the slaying of the firstborn in Egypt when the Jews were spared. The Presentation incorporates the dire prophecies of Simeon and Hannah.

Many portraits of the Spanish court present the figure of the sovereign standing beside a table, which often is draped in the Hapsburg colors of crimson and gold (Pl. 7). The appointment serves as an emblem for the priestly role of the king, a communicator of Christian ideology and defender of Catholic principles. Within a "dynastic" portrait, the table also drew an analogy between the king's consecration of his heir to God and St. Joseph's observance of the Mosaic law in the Temple of Jerusalem.[9] Numerous eighteenth- and nineteenth-century Mexican images portray the crowned figure of St. Joseph, holding the Christ Child and standing next to a table covered in the Hapsburg colors. This composition, echoing the royal portrait, may be a legacy of the custom of blending the image of the Spanish king with that of the earthly father of Christ (Catalogue 2).

PLATE 4.
Diego Quispe Tito (Peru), *Aries: St. Joseph and the Virgin Searching for an Inn*, 1681. Cathedral of Cuzco (Luis Enrique Tord).

The court of Philip III was particularly attuned to Josephine metaphors. In the redecoration of the Pardo Palace after a fire in March of 1604, a large gallery of Queen Margarita's apartments was decorated with a rich program of frescoes by Patricio Caxés (Pls. 8-10).[10] In *quadro riporte*, the ceiling presented panels which concerned the Old Testament "Story of Joseph." By the chamber's proximity to Philip III's quarters, the chamber's decoration suggested a tripartite correspondence among: the patriarch Joseph, regarded in medieval theology as a prefiguration of Christ; St. Joseph, the first follower of Christianity—which would supersede Judaism; and the king, whose descendants would be blessed by God.[11]

In Titian's *Allegory of Lepanto*, Prince Ferdinand's destiny to achieve apotheosis as a *Christomimetes* (Christ-imitator) is revealed by the impressive Victory and words *MAIORI TIBI*—"Greater things to you." Thus, the painting provided a time sequence underlying the sobriquet of Philip II as "*El Rey Prudente.*" The sobriquet and solar symbolism of the "rising" son have a *locus classicus* in the writings not only of Plato and Plutarch, but also of Hermes Trimegistus, who associated the Egyptian Serapis with Prudence. Plato discussed Prudence as a wise employer of the past, present and future, and Petrarch related time to the Graeco-Roman Apollo.[12]

PLATE 5.

Titian, *Allegory of Lepanto*, 1573-75. Prado Museum, Madrid.

The Flemish artist Justius Tiel portrayed *Prince Philip*, the future Philip III, in an iconographically complex portrait of 1590 (Pl. 11).[13] To the left of the young prince is a female with a sword, balance and caduceus. She can be identified as Astraea, goddess of justice and harbinger of the "Golden Age" foretold by Virgil.[14] The crowned figure of an old man behind her is "Father Time." With his arm he pushes Cupid to the side. The son of Venus symbolizes the corrupting influence of love upon heroes. The presence of these protective mythological personae in Tiel's portrait provides mutations of two popular Renaissance themes: *Veritas Filia Temporis*, or Truth unveiled by Time; and Innocence defended by Time and Justice.[15]

Florentine Neoplatonists significantly had perceived that a correspondence existed between Virgil's Astraea and Minerva, the ancient Roman goddess of wisdom and enlightenment. Inspired by Emperor Constantine's Messianic interpretations of Virgil's *Fourth Eclogue*, they equated Astraea's return to a corrupted earth with the advent of the Virgin Mary and the incarnation of an *Oriens Sol*.[16]

An *Oración* by Juan García de Becerril was presented in 1588 to the future Philip III. The text reflects upon the immortal glory which would be achieved by a union of arms and letters, heeding the sage advice of Minerva and following the prudence and good counsel of the Prince's father.[17] The allegorical figures in Tiel's portrait also may allude to his parents, Philip II and Queen Ana of Austria.

If in Tiel's portrait, the armed female encompasses a highly symbolical quartet (Astraea, Minerva, the Virgin Mary and Queen Ana), then the old crowned man assumes a quadripartite association with: the Iron Age Kronos supplanted by Astraea; the Plotinian Saturn, revealer of truth and counterpart of Minerva; St. Joseph, usually represented prior to the Council of Trent as an old man; and King Philip II, hailed as "*El Rey Prudente.*"

Catholic Spain perceived Mary and Joseph to be the first educators of the young Christ in the prophecies of the Old Testament (Pl. 12). Tiel's portrait of **Philip III** is a Platonic version of the Christian theme "The Holy House at Nazareth" (Catalogue 14). A royal prince was trained to be an imitator of Christ. This premise is the *raison d'être* for the manner in which the Prince of Asturias was depicted by Tiel. Philip III appears to be twelve, about the same age as that of Christ when debating with the Elders in the Temple. Attired in Hapsburg armor, he wears a crimson sash necklace with a pendant-insignia of the Order of the Golden Fleece.[18] Tiel's portrait implies, therefore, the future destiny of the royal scion. With the acquired virtues of justice and prudence, the young Philip III would effectively command a chivalric order of knighthood dedicated to the defense of Christian Truth.

PLATE 6.

Baltasar de Echave Orio (Mexico), *The Presentation in the Temple*, ca. 1615. Pinacoteca Virreinal, Mexico City.

A Carpenter's Staff of Authority, A King's Crown of Charity: Portraits of St. Joseph from Seville to the Americas

Analogies between the patriarch St. Joseph and the Spanish sovereign are oblique in court art of the sixteenth and seventeenth centuries. Beyond the metaphorical ambiance of Hapsburg Madrid, the cult of St. Joseph flourished, particularly due to the intercession of the Carmelite St. Teresa of Ávila and the publication of a treatise on Joseph written in 1597 by a Spanish Discalced Carmelite, Jerónimo Gracián de la Madre de Dios.[19] Gracián wrote that Joseph was the man most like Christ in countenance, speech and complexion. This contemplative, *vir* image was adopted by El Greco in his 1604 altarpiece for the Carmelite Church of St. Joseph in Toledo (Wilson, Pl. 3).[20] The feast day of St. Joseph, March 19, was decreed a holyday of obligation by Gregory XV in 1621. Numerous icons of Joseph were commissioned during the Spanish Golden Age, particularly by monastic orders in Andalusia.

Between 1635 and 1640, for the Sevillan Monastery of Discalced Mercedarians, Zurbarán represented *Saint Joseph Walking with the Child Jesus* (Wilson, Pl. 4).[21] The subject probably originated with Luke's description (2:41) of the Holy Family's journey to Jerusalem for the commemoration of Passover. To ecclesiastics and laymen, the theme may have served a didactic purpose by affirming the need to attend Church.

In another painting by Zurbarán, *The Flight into Egypt*, of 1636-1640 for the Sevillan Monastery of the Trinidad Calzada, Joseph and Mary are attired in Andalusian travelling clothes (Pl. 13).[22] Joseph is given prominence because he is silhouetted against a landscape and gestures eloquently towards his family. More iconic, perhaps because of the subject, Zurbarán's *The Coronation of St. Joseph, circa* 1636, focuses upon the heavenly rewards bestowed on Joseph for his piety and devotion (Pl. 14).[23]

After 1650, due to the gentler renditions of religious figures by the Sevillan Bartolomé Esteban Murillo, Spain tended to prefer a mellower type of Joseph, at once affectionate and empathetic. Murillo's *Holy Family with the Little Bird*, created prior to 1650, captures the emotional warmth of Joseph attending to his son in the house at Nazareth (Pl. 15).[24] Joseph watches over Christ, who instinctively shields a goldfinch, an emblem of the soul, from the danger of a dog's play. The spinning wheel in the background alludes to the beginning of the redemption "tapestry" and to the shroud of the Passion.

Religious art in the Americas was commissioned to assist the Catholic Church in the conversion of Indians. The encounter between Spain and the New World resulted in a grafting of European ideas and images to a pre-Columbian cultural tradition.[25] Created by several sophisticated societies that once flourished in Peru, Bolivia and Ecuador, ancient textiles and ceramics were characterized by complex patterns, bold colors, and abstract motifs that conceptualized the heavenly macrocosm and earthly microcosm (Pl. 16).[26] The practice of depicting symbols in antiquity was sustained in the post-Conquest. The originality and skill of Viceregal Indian artists is proven by their veiled allusions to Inca customs.

PLATE 8. Spanish School, *The Pardo Palace*, early 17th century. The Escorial Palace-Monastery (J. Miguel Morn Turina and Fernando Checa Cremades).

Indians of the New World initially had been taught how to paint by the early missionaries, who used engravings and book illustrations to communicate Christian imagery. By the late sixteenth century, European artists travelled to South America, bringing a knowledge of Italian and Flemish Mannerism.[27] Until a dispute of 1688, Andean Indian artists belonged to a guild established according to Spanish ordinances; by 1704 they had completely withdrawn from the system.[28] From this date, painters in Cuzco and Potosí (Alto Perú, present-day Bolivia) adopted a more archaic mode of painting.

By reverting to a decorative manner of representing forms, artists maintained a separation from contemporary European styles and defined their heritage. They deliberately stereotyped their compositions, ignored correct anatomy, proper lighting and rules of perspective. Andean artists intentionally overlaid their paintings with *brocateado*, gilded ornamentation achieved by using stencils (Pl. 17).[29] The conventional type of painting that resulted departed drastically from the "European" view of a natural world. Indian artists freely depicted flora and fauna of their native environment to recall an ancient artistic heritage.

PLATE 9.
The Queen's Gallery with Old Testament History of Joseph. The Pardo Palace (Patrimonio Nacional de España).

The scope of Colonial paintings of St. Joseph ranges from hieratic icons to narrative paintings of the childhood of Christ designed to evoke feelings of empathy. The theme of the "House of Nazareth" celebrated Joseph as a carpenter. Angels were portrayed aiding the Holy Family in domestic chores. Erecting Colonial buildings in Cuzco, Lima, Potosí, Quito and other centers, indigenous builders could identify with a saint who did manual labor in the service of God.

Viceregal Peru elevated the image of St. Joseph because his attribute of the flowering staff evoked the Inca legend about the founding of the sacred city of Cuzco. This attribute was derived from the legend that when the Virgin Mary was fourteen years old and was to be married, her suitors came to the temple, each with a wooden rod. Joseph's rod miraculously burst into bloom, indicating that he was the one favored by God to be the husband of Mary. Ancient myth recounts that Inti, son of the creator-god Viracocha, sent his children—Manco Capac (the Sun) and Mama Ocllo (the Moon)—to wander the Andes with a "golden wand."[30] Viracocha instructed them to build a city wherever the rod sank totally into the earth with a single thrust. The staff sank partially at *Pacarec Tampu*, the "Inn of the Dawn." Journeying further north, Manco Capac was able to plunge the "golden wand" into the ground. At this site rose the city of Cuzco, built in the shape of the puma, a solar beast.

St. Joseph undertook several journeys as a protector of Christ: the visit to Elizabeth and Zacharias, the voyage from Nazareth to Bethlehem, the flight into Egypt, the return from Egypt, and visits from Nazareth to Jerusalem at the time of Passover. In the Viceregal Andes, where journeys were made over perilous terrain, St. Joseph was invoked as a replacement for Manco Capac. The agrarian Incas venerated the stars and planets; their rituals at the Temple of the Sun in Cuzco centered upon nature and the fecundity of the earth during planting harvesting seasons.[31] Often Joseph was portrayed with flowers, emblems of divine favor and the earth's abundance (Wilson, Pl. 10).

By comparison with Viceregal South America, the art of New Spain—Mexico and Guatemala—stylistically was more realistic (Pls. 18 and 19).[32] Bonds with Seville were stronger, and Mexican painters retained European traditions of perspective, use of light, and selections of colors. Unlike the Andes, where *brocateado* masked the tangible and recalled abstract designs of a pre-Columbian past, Mexican guilds and later, the eighteenth-century Academy of San Carlos, favored naturalistic forms and space. Still, the majority of retables had ornate gilded framework which went beyond Sevillan churches in their opulence.

PLATE 10.
Patricio Cáxes, *Detail of the Queen's Gallery: Joseph Embracing Benjamin*, 1607-12. The Pardo Palace.

Many Mexican and Guatemalan devotional images of St. Joseph have their origin in Spanish art of seventeenth-century Andalusia. However, the legacy of the Aztec veneration of the sun by pagan high priests may be detected in some of the icons of the crowned St. Joseph, bearing his rod covered with profusely abundant blooms. Sixteenth-century codices document that Aztec priests wore headdresses composed of a basketlike framework covered with bark paper, feathers and blossoms.[33] Imitating ancient deities associated with agriculture, such

PLATE 11.
Justius Tiel. *Allegory of the Education of Philip III, ca.* 1590. Prado Museum, Madrid.

as Xochipilli, god of springtime and flowers, the Aztec priests participated in solar rituals (Pl. 20). During the Colonial epoch, the Mexican pre-Columbian heritage particularly was evoked in singular portraits of men painted to commemorate their taking the vows of priesthood (Pl. 21).[34]

For the Catholic priests, who sought to evangelize in frontier regions beyond populated settlements of Mexico, the ideal model to emulate was St. Joseph, whose paternal nature and virtuous qualities merited the highest crown of heaven. If the religious orders promoted associations between Christ's earthly father, sovereigns of Spain, and ancient ancestors, they did so with the loftiest of purposes—to ensure the dedication of a "New Eden" to the tripartite glory of God, the Church and Crown.

PLATE 12.
School of Cuzco (Peru), *The Holy Family with St. John the Baptist, ca.* 1725. Monastery of Santa Rosa, Lima (Ricardo Estabridis Cardenas).

PLATE 13.
Francisco de Zurbarán, *The Flight Into Egypt, ca.* 1636-40. Musée de Beaux Arts, Besançon.

PLATE 14.
Francisco de Zurbarán, *The Coronation of St. Joseph*, 1636. Museo de Provincial Bellas Artes, Seville.

PLATE 15.
Bartolomé Esteban Murillo, *The Holy Family with the Bird, ca.* 1650. Prado Museum, Madrid.

PLATE 16.
School of Cuzco (Peru), *St. Joseph and the Christ Child, ca.* 1720. Private Collection, Lima.

PLATE 17.
Diego Quispe Tito (Peru), *Corpus Christi Procession with Inca Chief and Nobility, ca.* 1670. Museo de Arte Religioso, Cuzco.

PLATE 18.
Marcos Zapata (Peru), *The Visitation, ca.* 1720. Monasterio de Santa Catalina, Cuzco (Luis Enrique Tord).

PLATE 19.
Luis Berrueco (Mexico), *The Visitation, ca.* 1730. The Denver Art Museum, 1987.627.

PLATE 20.
Teotihuacán Fresco Fragment, Tetitla Site, *Xochipilli, ca.* 650. The Denver Art Museum, 1965.202.

PLATE 21.
Anonymous Mexico, *Friar Francisco de Santa Ana, ca.* 1770. Museo Nacional del Virreinato, Tepozotlán, Mexico.

Notes

1. This essay is dedicated to the memory of Robert Stroessner, who generously shared his knowledge and enabled me to acquire his library of Spanish American Colonial art.

2. See María Jesús Pérez Martín, *Margarita of Austria, reina de España* (Madrid, 1961); Maria Kusche, *Juan Pantoja de la Cruz* (Madrid, 1964); Leticia Sánchez, *El Monasterio de la Encarnación de Madrid en el siglo XVII* (Salamanca: Ediciones Escurialenses, 1986).

3. Parrasio's work was displayed during the reign of Philip IV (1621-1665) in a large western gallery of the Buen Retiro Palace. According to the inventory of the Buen Retiro collection (composed after the death of Charles II in 1701), the painting was described as "a birth with Venus in a pavilion." For a full discussion of Parrasio's allegorical allusions to the birth of Apollo-Sol, see my *Philip IV and the "Golden House" of the Buen Retiro: In the Tradition of Caesar*, 2 vols. (New York-London, 1986), pp. 180-84.

4. Heraclitus (Greek philosopher, *ca.* 500 B.C.), *Quaestiones Homericae,* 72, 4-8; 11-19, edited by Buffière, *Allégories d'Homme* (Paris, 1962). See also Barbara von Barghahn, "Imaging the Cosmic Goddess: Sacred Legends and Metaphors for Majesty," *Temples of Gold, Crowns of Silver: Reflections of Majesty in the Viceregal Americas,* edited by Barbara von Barghahn (Washington, D.C.: George Washington University, 1991), pp. 99-115.

5. See Luis Enrique Tord, "La serie del Zodíaco de Diego Quispe Tito," in *El Zodíaco en el Perú* (Lima, 1987), pp. 43-71 (58: St. Joseph and the Virgin Searching for an Inn); José de Mesa and Teresa Gisbert, "El Zodíaco del pintor indio Diego Quispe Tito," *Traza y Baza* (Barcelona), 1 (1972).

6. Jusepe Martinez, *Discourses practicables del nobilismo arte de la pintura,* edited by Valentín Carderera y Solano (Madrid, 1866) (Alonso Sánchez Coello's drawing sent to Titian). Also see Harold Wethey, *The Paintings of Titian, II* (The Portraits) (London, 1971), and Steven N. Orso, *Philip IV and the Decoration of the Alcázar of Madrid* (Princeton, 1986).

7. José Moreno, "Cómo son y cómo eran unas Tizianos del Prado," *Archivo español de arte y arqueología, 9* (1933), 113-16. A payment to Vicencio Carducho was issued on December 24, 1625 for restoration and enlargement of three large canvases in the new audience hall of the Alcázar (later known as the "Hall of Mirrors"). *The Allegory of Lepanto* (3.35 x 2.74 meters) was enlarged to serve as a pendant to Titian's *Equestrian Portrait of Charles V at the Battle of Mühlberg* (3.32 x 2.79 meters), a work in the Prado Museum. The bound Moor in the *Allegory of Lepanto* was added by Carducho in order to draw a comparison between Philip II and his father, Charles V. Carducho's source was Leone Leoni's 1548 bronze statue of *Charles V Vanquishing Fury* (Prado Museum). Leone's imposing statue of Charles V was cast with removable armor, although the nude figure of the Holy Roman Emperor was rarely displayed. The bronze Spanish Augustus victorious over a chained Fury was reproduced in several replicas for a twofold purpose: the image was a forceful symbol of monarchical authority in the milieu of the court; it elevated a dynastic patriarch from whom Hapsburg sovereigns could trace their ancestry to the Roman caesars and ultimately, to Aeneas.

8. Erwin Panofsky, *Problems in Titian, Mostly Iconographic,* The Wrightsman Lectures, New York University (New York, 1969), pp. 72-73.

9. To the best of my knowledge, this interpretation of the table in Hapsburg portraiture has not been suggested. For additional information about courtly portraits, see *Alonso Sánchez Coello y el retrato en la corte de Felipe II* (Madrid: Prado Museum, 1990).

10. See Manuel Ayala y Raya, *Real Sitio de El Pardo* (Madrid, 1983); Antonio Bonet Correa, *El Pardo,* (Madrid, 1980); Fernando Marías, "El Palacio Real de el Pardo de Carlos V a Felipe III," *Reales Sitios,* número extraordinario (1989), 137-46; Juan Miguel Morn and Fernando Checa Cremades, *Las casas del rey. Casas del campo, cazaderos y jardines. Siglos XVI y XVII* (Madrid, 1986). The Patrimonio Nacional kindly permitted me to view and photograph the Hapsburg wing of the Pardo during its restoration, including the "Queen's Gallery" decorated by Cáxes between 1607 and 1612.

11. Santiago Sebastián López , *El barroco iberoamericano* (Madrid, 1990), pp. 109-29, discusses the iconography of the sons of Jacob in Spain and the New World.

12. Panofsky, *Problems in Titian, Mostly Iconographic,* pp. 88-108.

13. *Catálogo de las pinturas. Museo del Prado* (Madrid, 1985), p. 678.

14. See Frances A. Yates, *Astrea: The Imperial Theme in the Sixteenth-Century* (London-Boston, 1975). Tiel's source for the image of Astraea was Angelo Bronzino. Erwin Panofsky, *Studies in Iconology: Humanistic Themes of the Renaissance* (1939; New York, 1972), illustrates a tapestry in the Galleria degli Arrazzi (Florence) by Giovanni Rost after Bronzino's *The Vindication of Innocence* (Pl. XXXV).

15. Panofsky, *Studies in Iconology,* pp. 69-94; and Fritz Saxl, *Veritas Filia Temporis: Philosophy and History. Essays Presented to Ernst Cassirer* (Oxford, 1936), pp. 197-222.

16. See Ernst H. Kantorowitz, "Oriens Augusti—Lever du Roi," *Dumbarton Oaks Papers,* no. 17, (Washington, D.C.), pp. 119-77.

17. Juan Miguel Serrera, "La mecánica del retrato de corte," in *Alonso Sánchez Coello y el retrato en la corte de Felipe II*, p. 41.

18. Philip III's armor is in the collection of the Metropolitan Museum of Art. For information about sixteenth-century armor, see José A. Godoy, "Renaissance Arms and Armor from the Patrimonio Nacional," in *Resplendence of the Spanish Monarchy: Renaissance Tapestries and Armor from the Patrimonio Nacional* (New York: Metropolitan Museum of Art, 1991), pp. 95-164.

19. See Christopher Wilson, "Beyond Strong Men and Frontiers: Conquests of the Spanish Mystics," in *Temples of Gold, Crowns of Silver,* pp. 116-27, and "St. Teresa of Ávila's Holy Patron: Teresian Sources for the Image of St. Joseph in Spanish American Colonial Art" in the present volume; Jerónimo Gracián de la Madre de Dios, *Josefina. Summario de las excelencias del glorioso S. Joseph, esposo de la Virgen María,* 1597 (1629 edition), folios 12, 138.

20. See Harold Wethey, *El Greco and His School,* 2 vols. (Princeton, 1962); and *El Greco of Toledo* (Washington, D.C.: National Gallery of Art, 1988). Richard Mann presented a comprehensive lecture on El Greco's paintings for the Toledan Church of St. Joseph at the conference "Spain and Portugal of the Navigators: The Iberian Peninsula Countries, Europe and New Horizons," September 25-30, 1990, George Washington University and Georgetown University. Also see his *El Greco and His Patrons: Three Major Projects* (Cambridge, 1986) for additional information about the intellectual climate of Toledo during the late sixteenth century.

21. Jean Baticle, *Zurbarán* (New York: Metropolitan Museum of Art, 1987), pp. 149-52.

22. *Ibid.,* pp. 123-25.

23. *The Coronation of St. Joseph* has been attributed to Bernarbé de Ayala, a follower of Zurbarán. See Julián Gállego and José Gudiol, *Zurbarán* (Barcelona, 1977), p. 97.

24. See Diego Ángulo Iñiguez, *Murillo,* 3 vols., II, 175-176; and catalogue section by Manuela Mena and Enrique Valdivieso, in *Murillo,* exhibition catalogue (Madrid: Prado Museum, and London: Royal Academy of Arts, 1982), pp. 158-59.

Alfonso E. Pérez Sánchez, *Pintura italiana del siglo VII en España* (Madrid, 1967), p. 229, has commented that a copy of Federico Barocci's *Madonna del Gatto* in Ecija (a province of Seville) may have been known to Murillo.

25. Barbara von Barghahn, "From the Tower of David to the Citadel of Solomon: Mirrors of Virtue for a Viceregal 'Silver Age'," in *Temples of Gold, Crowns of Silver*, pp. 154-79, provides an analysis of cult images such as the Virgin of Guadalupe (Mexico and the Andes), as well as colonial icons of the Virgin Mary that extol Queen Isabel the Catholic. See also *Gloria en Excelsis. The Virgin and Angels in Viceregal Paintings of Peru and Bolivia*, edited by Barbara Duncan (New York: Center for Inter-American Relations, 1986).

26. For information about the pre-Columbian legacy in the colonial Andes, see Teresa Gisbert, *Icongrafía y mitos indígenas en el arte* (La Paz, 1980), and "The Andean Gods through Christianity," in *Temples of Gold, Crowns of Silver*, pp. 80-92.

27. See Santiago Sebastián, "The Diffusion of Counter-Reformation Doctrine," in *Temples of Gold, Crowns of Silver*, pp. 57-79.

28. José de Mesa and Teresa Gisbert, *Historia de la pintura cuzqueña*, 2 vols. (1962; Lima, 1982)), I:137.

29. Barbara von Barghahn, "A Silver Age of Colonial Latin America: The Viceregal Andes and the Persistence of Tradition," *The 1992 Washington Antiques Show, Quincentennial Commemorative Catalogue* (Washington, D.C., 1992), pp. 101-107.

30. Felipe Guaman Poma de Ayala, *Nueva corónica y buen gobierno* (*circa* 1613) provides a comprehensive history of culture and customs of the ancient Inca. This text is available in a modern edition prepared by J. R. Murra (Mexico, 1980).

31. Barbara von Barghahn, "A Crucible of Gold: The 'Rising Sun' of Monarchy in the Blending of Cultures, in *Temples of Gold, Crowns of Silver*, pp. 34-56.

32. See Manuel Toussaint, *Colonial Art in Mexico*, translated and edited by Elizabeth Wilder Weismann, (Austin-London, 1967); *Mexico: Splendors of 30 Centuries* (New York: Metropolitan Museum of Art, 1991); Robert Stroessner, "Beyond the Pillars of Hercules: Spanish Colonial Painting from the New World," in *Temples of Gold, Crowns of Silver*, pp. 16-33.

33. Linda Bantel and Marcus Burke, *Spain and New Spain: Mexican Colonial Arts in the European Context* (Corpus Chrisit: Art Museum of South Texas, 1979), p. 115.

34. Also consult *Monjas Coronadas* (Artes de Mexico, 1960), particularly Rogelio Ruiz Gomar, "Retratos de Monjas," pp. 24-51 and Graciela Romandía de Cantú, "Vida Conventual," pp. 68-94.

Catalogue of the Exhibition

1. Antonio de Torres (Mexico).
   St. Joseph with the Christ Child.
   18th century.
   Oil on canvas.
   38" x 26 ½".
   Private Collection, Massachusetts.

2. Mexican.
   St. Joseph with the Christ Child.
   19th century.
   Oil on tin.
   14" x 10".
   Private Collection, Virginia.

3. Miguel Cabrera (Mexico).
   St. Joseph with the Christ Child.
   18th century.
   Oil on copper.
   22" x 16 ½".
   Private Collection, Virginia.

4. Mexican.
   St. Joseph with the Christ Child.
   Late 18th-early 19th century.
   Oil on canvas, mounted on wood panel.
   15" x 10".
   Private Collection, Pennsylvania.

5. Mexican.
   St. Joseph with the Christ Child.
   19th century.
   Oil on tin.
   14" x 10".
   Private Collection, Pennsylvania.

6. School of Cuzco (Peru).
   St. Joseph with the Christ Child.
   18th century.
   Oil on canvas.
   39 ½" x 25".
   Private Collection, Virginia.

7. School of Cuzco (Peru).
   The Nativity with Angels.
   17th century.
   Oil on canvas.
   46 ½" x 37".
   Private Collection, Virginia.

8. School of Collao (Region now divided between Peru and Bolivia, adjacent Lake Titicaca).
   Marriage of the Virgin and St. Joseph.
   17th century.
   Oil on canvas.
   29" x 47"
   Private Collection, Washington, D.C.

9. School of Collao (Region now divided between Peru and Bolivia, adjacent Lake Titicaca).
   The Flight into Egypt.
   17th century.
   Oil on canvas.
   29" x 47".
   Private Collection, Washington, D.C.

10. School of Cuzco (Peru).
    St. Joseph with the Christ Child.
    18th century.
    Oil on canvas.
    25 ¼" x 18 ½".
    Private Collection, Virginia.

11. School of Cuzco (Peru).
    St. Joseph Walking with the Christ Child.
    18th century.
    Oil on canvas.
    37" x 29 1/2".
    Private Collection, Washington, D.C.

12. School of Collao (Region now divided between Peru and Bolivia, adjacent Lake Titicaca).
    The Heavenly and Earthly Trinities.
    18th century.
    Oil on canvas.
    27" x 21".
    Private Collection, Washington, D.C.

13. Manuel de Samaniego (Ecuador).
    The Rest on the Flight into Egypt.
    18th century.
    Oil on canvas.
    15" x 19".
    Private Collection, Washington, D.C.

14. Manuel de Samaniego (Ecuador).
    The Holy House at Nazareth.
    18th century.
    Oil on canvas.
    15" x 19".
    Private Collection, Washington, D.C.

15. School of Potosí (Bolivia).
    Retable with St. Joseph and the Christ Child.
    18th century.
    Polychromed wood.
    29 1/2" x 17 1/2" x 12".
    The Art Museum of the Americas, Washington, D.C.

BIOBIBLIOGRAPHICAL NOTES

Joseph F. Chorpenning, O.S.F.S.

St. Teresa of Ávila (as she is known in the English-speaking world) or **Teresa of Jesus** was born in the medieval walled, fortress-like city of Ávila on March 28, 1515. On her father's side, she was of Jewish descent. Her paternal grandfather, a *converso* or converted Jew, had been reconciled by the Inquisition for maintaining practices of the Jewish religion after his conversion to Christianity. Teresa was reared in a close-knit family that enjoyed reading, and hence at any early age she began to read the lives of the saints and chivralric romances. After her mother's death in 1528, Teresa was sent to the Augustinian nuns' convent school of Our Lady of Grace that was located just outside Ávila. There she began to consider a religious vocation. Her reading of the *Letters of St. Jerome* was pivotal in her decision to enter the Carmelite monastery of the Incarnation in Ávila in 1535. After an initial period of peace and contentment, Teresa lost her first fervor. In her autobiography Teresa describes her life over the next two decades as a constant conflict and battle between friendship with God and friendship with the world. In 1554 Teresa, moved by an image of the wounded Christ (an *Ecce Homo*) before which she was praying and by her reading of St. Augustine's *Confessions*, experienced a conversion. From this point on, Teresa strove diligently to practice prayer regularly and to avoid all that would distract her from it. As a result, she began to be granted various mystical favors, in the course of which she discerned a divine mission to reform the Carmelites by reclaiming their primitive charism of constant prayer, solitude and silence, and strict poverty. Teresa founded the first reformed monastery of St. Joseph in Ávila on August 24, 1562. Over the next twenty years, she would found sixteen more monasteries all over Spain, enduring harsh Castilian winters and Andalusian summers in order to do so. Teresa named twelve of the seventeen monasteries she founded for St. Joseph. Teresa's reform of the Carmelite nuns served as the catalyst for a reform of the friars as well; Teresa's closest and most faithful collaborator in the latter endeavor was St. John of the Cross. During this period she also wrote prolifically. The extant corpus of her writings includes some 450 letters, poetry, a number of short prose works, and her four major prose works: the *Book of Her Life* (begun in 1562 and completed in 1565), her autobiography; *Way of Perfection* (probably written in 1566), the manifesto of the Teresian reform; *Interior Castle* (1577), Teresa's masterwork that charts the evolution of the spiritual life from the recovery of one's true identity as a creature made in God's image and likeness to the spiritual marriage of God and the soul; and *Book of Her Foundations* (begun in 1573 and completed in 1582), the chronicle of the dissemination of the Teresian Carmel. Teresa died, probably of cancer of the uterus, on October 4, 1582 in Alba de Tormes, where she is buried. The Gregorian calendar went into effect the next day, and thus the day of her death became October 15, the date of her feast day in the liturgical calendar. Teresa was beatified on April 24, 1614, and canonized eight years later, on March 12, 1622, together with her fellow Spaniards Ignatius Loyola, Isidore of Madrid, Francis Xavier, and the Italian Philip Neri. On September 27, 1970 Pope Paul VI declared Teresa the first woman Doctor of the Church.

The classic modern English translation of Teresa's works is that of E. Allison Peers: *The Complete Works of St. Teresa of Jesus*, 3 vols. (1946; London: Sheed and Ward, 1978), and *The Letters of St. Teresa of Jesus*, 2 vols. (1951; London: Sheed and Ward, 1980). A more recent, and smooth-reading, translation is that of Kieran Kavanaugh, O.C.D., and Otilio Rodríguez, O.C.D.: *The Collected Works of St. Teresa of Ávila*, 3 vols. (Washington, D.C.: Institute of Carmelite Studies, 1976-85). The latter translation also contains excellent introductions by

Fr. Kavanaugh to each of the works translated. There is a huge body of secondary literature on Teresa. The celebration in 1982 of the fourth centenary of Teresa's death not only added to this corpus but has served as a catalyst for a widespread renewal of interest at both the popular and scholarly levels in the Mother of Carmel. Books in the English language on Teresa published since the 1982 quatercentenary include: Jodi Bilinkoff, *The Ávila of St. Teresa: Religious Reform in a Sixteenth-Century City* (Ithaca: Cornell University Press, 1989), a historical analysis of Teresa's reform in its social and religious context; Joseph F. Chorpenning, O.S.F.S., *The Divine Romance: Teresa of Ávila's Narrative Theology* (Chicago: Loyola University Press, 1992), a commentary on Teresa's four major prose works that can be read alongside her original texts; Alison Weber, *Teresa of Ávila and the Rhetoric of Femininity* (Princeton: Princeton University Press, 1990), a socio-linguistic study of the rhetorical strategy of Teresa's four major prose works; and Rowan Williams, *Teresa of Ávila* (Wilton, Connecticut: Morehouse Publishing, 1991), an introduction to Teresa's life and works that makes use of the most recent historical research on Teresa and her society.

St. Francis de Sales was born in the Château de Sales at Thorens in Savoy, a region in southeastern France on the borders of Italy and Switzerland, on August 21, 1567. He received his early education at the College of La Roche, where young nobles and bourgeois were educated, and at the Capuchin College in Annecy. In 1578 Francis was sent to the Jesuit College of Clermont in Paris to study humanities and philosophy. While there he also took lessons in horseback riding, dancing, and fencing—social graces a young man of his noble status was expected to acquire. In 1586 he was assailed by an agonizing temptation to despair of his salvation. Francis was delivered from this trial in January 1587 as he prayed the *Memorare* before the statue of the Black Virgin in the Dominican church of Saint Étienne des Grès in Paris. After receiving the licentiate and master of arts degrees in Paris and after returning to his native Savoy for a brief visit with his family, Francis went to Padua, where he studied law to please his father and theology to please himself. Upon his arrival in Padua, Francis' primary concern was to find a spiritual director. He placed himself under the direction of the Jesuit Antonio Possevino, a renowned humanist and diplomat, who inculcated in Francis the universal, cosmopolitan, and catholic outlook that would become one of the saint's hallmarks. Under Possevino's guidance, Francis composed a rule of life, entitled *Spiritual Exercises*, to assist him in cultivating his spiritual life in the midst of the dissipated world of student life in which he found himself. In 1592 Francis received his doctorate in law. On his return to Savoy, he announced that he had discerned a vocation to the priesthood. To mollify his father's opposition to this decision, it was arranged for Francis to assume the position of provost of the cathedral chapter of Geneva. (Due to the Calvinist occupation of Geneva, the Catholic Bishop of Geneva was forced to reside in Annecy.) Francis was ordained a priest on December 18, 1593. He spent the next four years laboring to convert the Chablais region back to Catholicism. During this period he composed two works of apologetic character: the *Catholic Controversy* and *Defense of the Standard of the Holy Cross*. In 1599 Francis was appointed coadjutor to the Bishop of Geneva, and on December 8, 1602, he was consecrated Bishop of Geneva. Francis was a model bishop who tirelessly devoted himself to preaching, hearing confessions, teaching catechism, administering his diocese, giving spiritual direction, and writing. In 1609 his most popular and well-known book, the *Introduction to the Devout Life*, which grew out of letters of instruction and advice that he wrote to a young female cousin who lived at court, was published. This was followed by his masterpiece of mystical theology, the *Treatise on the Love of God*, that appeared in 1616. In 1610 Francis founded with St. Jane Frances de Chantal, whom he first met in 1604 while preaching a series of Lenten sermons in Dijon, the order of the Visitation of Holy Mary. It was to these early Visitandines that Francis gave his famous *Spiritual Conferences*. Francis died of a cerebral hemorrhage on December 28, 1622 at Lyons. His body is buried in the basilica of the

Visitation monastery in Annecy. He was beatified on December 28, 1661, and canonized on April 19, 1665. At the time of his canonization, his feast day was assigned to January 29, the day of his burial. With the reform of the liturgical calendar after Vatican II, it was reassigned to January 24, the day of the solemn transferral of his body from Lyons to Annecy. Pope Pius IX declared Francis a Doctor of the Church on July 7, 1877. In his encyclical *Rerum Omnium* that commemorated the third centenary of Francis' death, Pope Pius XI proclaimed Francis the patron of journalists and Catholic writers.

In the edition of his complete works published by the Annecy Visitation (1892-1932), Francis' extant writings comprise twenty-six volumes. Modern English translations of most of Francis' major works are available: *The Catholic Controversy*, translated by Henry Benedict Mackey, O.S.B. (1886; Rockford, Illinois: Tan Books, 1989); *Introduction to the Devout Life*, translated by John K. Ryan (1972; New York: Image Books, 1989); *Treatise on the Love of God*, translated by John K. Ryan, 2 vols. (1963; Rockford, Illinois: Tan Books, 1974-75); *The Spiritual Conferences of St. Francis de Sales*, translated by F. Aidan Gasquet, O.S.B., and Henry Benedict Mackey, O.S.B. (1906; Westminster, Maryland: Newman Press, 1962); *Selected Letters*, translated by Elisabeth Stopp (New York: Harper, 1960); Francis de Sales and Jane de Chantal, *Letters of Spiritual Direction*, translated by Péronne Marie Thibert, V.H.M., The Classics of Western Spirituality (New York: Paulist Press, 1988); *The Sermons of St. Francis de Sales, I: On Prayer; II: On Our Lady; III: For Lent Given in 1622; IV: For Advent and Christmas*, translated by Nuns of the Visitation and edited by Lewis S. Fiorelli, O.S.F.S., 4 vols. (Rockford, Illinois: Tan Books, 1985-87). The classic study of Francis' life and writings is E. J. Lajeunie's masterful intellectual biography *St. Francis de Sales: The Man, The Thinker, His Influence*, translated by Rory O' Sullivan, O.S.F.S., 2 vols. (Bangalore, India: St. Francis de Sales Publications, 1986-87). A shorter biography is André Ravier, *Francis de Sales: Sage and Saint*, translated by Joseph D. Bowler, O.S.F.S. (San Francisco: Ignatius Press, 1988). An indispensable study of Francis' education at Clermont College is Elisabeth Stopp, "St. Francis de Sales at Clermont College: A Humanist Education in Sixteenth-Century Paris," *Salesian Studies*, 6, no. 1 (Winter 1969), 42-63. Several excellent publications on Francis by Wendy M. Wright provide a reliable introduction to his spirituality and merit enthusiastic recommendation: "François de Sales: Gentleness and Civility," in *The Spirituality of Western Christendom, II: The Roots of the Modern Christian Tradition*, edited by E. Rozanne Elder (Kalamazoo: Cistercian Publications, 1984), pp. 124-44; *Bond of Perfection: Jeanne de Chantal & François de Sales* (New York: Paulist Press, 1985); (with Joseph F. Power, O.S.F.S.) "Introduction" to Francis de Sales and Jane de Chantal, *Letters of Spiritual Direction*, translated by Péronne Marie Thibert, V.H.M., The Classics of Western Spirituality (New York: Paulist Press, 1988), pp. 9-86; and "'That is what it is made for': The Image of the Heart in the Spirituality of Francis de Sales and Jane de Chantal," in *Spiritualities of the Heart: Approaches to Personal Wholeness in the Christian Tradition*, edited by Annice Callahan (New York: Paulist Press, 1990), pp. 143-58.

SUGGESTIONS FOR FURTHER READING

Christopher Chadwick Wilson

This list includes only publications in English. For a comprehensive bibliography on Spanish American Colonial art, with references to important foreign language texts, see *Temples of Gold, Crowns of Silver*, pp. 183-89.

Arenal, Electa, and Stacy Schlau. *Untold Sisters: Hispanic Nuns in Their Own Works.* Albuquerque: University of New Mexico Press, 1989.

Bantel, Linda, and Marcus Burke. *Spain and New Spain: Mexican Colonial Arts in Their European Context.* Corpus Christi: Art Museum of South Texas, 1979.

Barghahn, Barbara von. *Age of Gold, Age of Iron: Renaissance Spain and Symbols of Monarchy.* 2 vols. Lanham, Maryland: University Press of America, 1985.

Barghahn, Barbara von, *et al. Temples of Gold, Crowns of Silver: Reflections of Majesty in the Viceregal Americas.* Washington, D.C.: George Washington University, 1991.

Brown, Jonathan. *The Golden Age of Painting in Spain.* New Haven: Yale University Press, 1991.

Castedo, Leopoldo. *The Cuzco Circle.* New York: Center for Inter-American Relations, 1976.

Enrique Tord, Luis, *et al. Gloria in Excelsis: The Virgin and Angels in Viceregal Painting of Peru and Bolivia.* New York: Center for Inter-American Relations, 1986.

Filas, Francis L., S.J. *The Man Nearest to Christ: Nature and Historic Development of the Devotion to St. Joseph.* Milwaukee: Bruce Publishing Company, 1944.

—. *Joseph Most Just: Theological Questions about St. Joseph.* Milwaukee: Bruce Publishing Company, 1956.

Giffords, Gloria Fraser, *et al. The Art of Private Devotion: Retablo Painting of Mexico.* Fort Worth: InterCultura, and Dallas: The Meadows Museum, 1991.

Goodpasture, H. McKennie, editor. *Cross and Sword: An Eyewitness History of Christianity in Latin America.* Maryknoll, New York: Orbis, 1989.

Keleman, Pal. *Baroque and Rococo in Latin America.* New York: Dover, 1967.

—. *Peruvian Colonial Painting: A Special Exhibition.* New York: The Brooklyn Museum, 1971.

Kubler, George, and Martin S. Soria. *Art and Architecture in Spain and Portugal and Their American Dominions, 1500-1800.* Pelican History of Art. Baltimore: Penguin Books, 1959.

Palmer, Gabrielle G. *Sculpture in the Kingdom of Quito.* Albuquerque: University of New Mexico Press, 1987.

Patrignani, Anthony-Joseph, S.J. *A Manual of Practical Devotion to the Glorious Patriarch St. Joseph.* Translated and revised by a Member of the Society of Jesus. 1865. Rockford, Illinois: Tan Books, 1982.

Stein, Susan T. *The Tapestry of St. Joseph: Chronological History of St. Joseph and His Apostle, Blessed Brother André.* Philadelphia: Apostle Publishing, 1991.

Toussaint, Manuel. *Colonial Art in Mexico.* Translated and edited by E. Wilder Weismann. Austin: University of Texas Press, 1967.

Contributors and Exhibition Curators

Barbara von Barghahn received her M.A. and Ph.D. degrees in art history from the Institute of Fine Arts, New York University. Presently she is associate professor of art history at George Washington University in Washington, D.C. Her publications include the books *Philip IV and the "Golden House" of the Buen Retiro*, 2 vols. (New York: Garland Press, 1986) and *Age of Gold, Age of Iron: Renaissance Spain and Symbols of Monarchy*, 2 vols. (Lanham, Maryland: University Press of America, 1986), as well as articles in scholarly journals and exhibition catalogues. Recently Dr. von Barghahn was guest curator of the exhibition "Temples of Gold, Crowns of Silver: Reflections of Majesty in the Viceregal Americas" at the Art Museum of the Americas, Organization of American States, and the George Washington University Dimock Gallery, both in Washington, D.C. Currently she is preparing two exhibitions sponsored by The Trust for Museum Exhibitions: "Goya: *Caprichos, Disasters of the War, Tauromaquia, Disparates* (1992) and "Beyond the Pillars of Hercules: Viceregal Paintings of the New World" (1993).

Joseph F. Chorpenning is a priest of the Congregation of the Oblates of St. Francis de Sales. He has a Ph.D. in Hispanic Studies from Johns Hopkins and an S.T.L., with a specialization in the history of spirituality, from Catholic University of America. He has published a critical edition of a collection of sixteenth-century Spanish religious poetry (Exeter University Press, 1977) and over two dozen articles on, among other topics, St. Teresa of Ávila, St. Francis de Sales, Caravaggio, and Henri Nouwen, in various journals, including *Bulletin of Hispanic Studies, Spirituality Today, Carmelite Studies,* and *The Downside Review.* His book *The Divine Romance: Teresa of Ávila's Narrative Theology* will be published this spring by Loyola University Press in Chicago. Fr. Chorpenning is a member of the editorial board of *Studia Mystica* and of the series "Medieval and Early Modern Mysticism" published by Peter Lang. Currently Fr. Chorpenning is Assistant to the President at St. Joseph's University.

Santiago Sebastián López is an internationally renowned Spanish art historian. Professor of art history at the University of Valencia in Spain, he is founding editor of the journal *Traza y Baza: Cuadernos Hispanos de Simbología.* He has published numerous journal articles, exhibition catalogues, and books, including *Espacio y símbolo* (1976), *Mensaje del arte medieval* (1978), *Arte y humanismo* (1978), *La clave del "Guernica"* (1981), *Contrarreforma y barroco: Lecturas iconográficas e iconológicas* (1981; 2nd edition, 1985), (with José de Mesa and Teresa Gisbert) *Arte iberoamericano*, vols. 28 and 29 of the collection *Summa Artis* (1985), *"El fisiólogo" atribuido a San Epifanio* (1986), and *El barroco iberoamericano: Mensaje iconográfico* (1990).

Christopher Chadwick Wilson has a B.A. in art history from the University of South Carolina and an M.A. in art history from George Washington University. Presently he is a Ph.D. candidate at George Washington. Mr. Wilson has presented papers on Spanish American Colonial art at the two-part international conference "Portugal and Spain of the Navigators: The Age of Exploration," held in September 1990 at Georgetown University and in January 1992 at George Washington University. His essay "Beyond Strong Men and Frontiers: Conquests of the Spanish Mystics" was published in *Temples of Gold, Crowns of Silver: Reflections of Majesty in the Viceregal Americas,* edited by Barbara von Barghahn (George Washington University, 1991).

4760